Enough!

Federalist No. 86

Enough!

Fixing the Foundation of America's Destiny

by Publius MMX

RECOVERING FEDERALIST, LLC

ISBN 978-0-9845512-2-4

Printed in the United States of America.

All that is necessary for the triumph of evil
is for good men to do nothing.

—*Edmund Burke*

Contents

Foreword

Freedom is not a gift bestowed upon us by other men, but a right that belongs to us by the laws of God and nature.

Benjamin Franklin

This will be the best security for maintaining our liberties. A nation of well-informed men who have been taught to know and prize the rights which God has given them cannot be enslaved. It is in the religion of ignorance that tyranny begins.

Benjamin Franklin

The germ of dissolution of our federal government is in the constitution of the federal judiciary: an irresponsible body, (for impeachment is scarcely a scare-crow,) working like gravity by night and by day, gaining a little to-day and a little tomorrow, and advancing its noiseless step like a thief, over the field of jurisdiction until all shall be usurped from the States, and the government of all be consolidated into one. To this I am opposed; because, when all government, domestic and foreign, in little as in great things, shall be drawn to Washington as the centre of all it will render powerless the checks provided of one government on another and will become as venal and oppressive as the government from which we separated.

Thomas Jefferson

The Constitution is not an instrument for the government to restrain the people, it is an instrument for the people to restrain the government—lest it come to dominate our lives and interests.

Patrick Henry

We are not weak if we make a proper use of those means which the God of Nature has placed in our power … the battle, sir, is not to the strong alone it is to the vigilant, the active, the brave.

Patrick Henry

Is life so dear or peace so sweet as to be purchased at the price of chains and slavery? Forbid it, Almighty God! I know not what course others may take, but as for me, give me liberty, or give me death!

Patrick Henry

Acknowledgments

First of all, we acknowledge and recognize the laws of nature and nature's God.

We acknowledge divine providence and its hand in all things, including this effort. We understand that others may not, but regardless of whether we believe in God, lessons from history, manifest destiny, karma, or just plain ol' dumb luck, if we deny the laws of nature and their existence, we do so at our own peril—individually and collectively. We not only recognize those laws, but also acknowledge a guiding hand in this work.

We also wish to acknowledge and recognize the founders of this great nation and those who framed the original debates—the Federalist/Anti-Federalist debate and other important debates that we desire to reignite with this work. We are truly concerned about our country and believe that time is of the essence for this discussion, which will continue with ongoing essays, books, and other works produced by Publius MMX, Recovering Federalist.

The Pen is Mightier than the Sword!

Preface

This essay is part of the *Federalist No. 86* series, a continuation of the discussion we began with *Bedrock!—Federalist No. 86*. The preface and general introduction to this whole discussion is contained there. That essay also helps provide the foundation and set the stage for this and other essays, including *Prosperity!*, a companion essay to this one that focuses on the economy and on government financial matters. Both of those essays reexamine the original Federalist/Anti-Federalist debate and relevant issues in the context of two hundred-plus years of history and applied theory.

This essay fully recognizes that the laws of nature and personal responsibility, as discussed in *Bedrock!*, are the foundation of our existence. But the focus of this essay turns from what we can and should be doing as individuals at the foundational level to what we can and must do as a country to correct our course.

We don't pretend to be scholars, constitutional or otherwise. The primary source of our education has been in the school of hard knocks. Rather than discuss abstract theory in this essay, we will talk mostly about our observations in the everyday world—our own experiences and those of others who have contributed stories and experiences to this cause, including Worth Woolsey, Mancos MacLeod, Matt James, Maggie Rawlins, Rosie McLayne, Nick Romero, Doug Ketchum, Charlie Adams, and others who have provided real-life stories for this essay and the others we are working on. In all cases, the stories are real, but in some cases two or more stories have been blended, and the names and places have been changed to protect the privacy of and provide anonymity for the parties involved.

Once again, our focus is on principles, not personalities. Likewise in this essay, instead of discussing what Band-Aids can be put on symptoms to ignore core causes and push them forward for someone else to attempt to address and resolve, we address the core systemic issues and structural reforms that must occur in order to fix the foundation of American Government, correct course, and fulfill America's intended divine destiny.

Introduction and Background

The U.S. Constitution was approved by the Constitutional Convention on September 17, 1787. As described in *Bedrock!* and elsewhere, from the time the Constitution was signed by the delegates at the convention to the time it was finally ratified by the last state (Rhode Island) in 1790, a fierce national debate—the Federalist / Anti-Federalist Debate—raged in the states regarding this great American experiment—the Constitution—and the new government it was intended to create. This debate occurred in meeting halls, on streets, and on the printed page. On both sides, heated discussion was the order of the day, and both sides had a considerable following.

Final ratification of the Constitution essentially ended the formal Federalist / Anti-Federalist Debate. It is our position, however, that the debate has never really ended. It ebbs and flows, waxes, wanes and simmers at times, but many of the questions raised at that time have never been fully resolved, and remain with us today: How should society be ordered? What is the proper role of government? What is the best form of government? What rights must governments protect? Which government powers should be held by the states, and which ones by the federal government? How can governments best be held accountable and in check? Many of these questions seem to be particularly salient right now.

One big difference between our situation today and that of the original Federalists is that they had the connections and resources to launch a massive PR campaign and completely dominate the discussion. By publishing the *Federalist Papers* in the main newspapers available in the colonies at the time, they had an absolute corner on the ability to communicate and spread their message, giving them a big lead and an unquestionable advantage in the Federalist/Anti-Federalist public relations campaign. Given that there were limited sources of public information at the time—word of mouth and newspapers and other publications—participating in that debate was in some ways much simpler than participating in similar debates now. On the other hand, many of the Anti-Federalist essays and rebuttals that were submitted for publication were never even published at the time. Consequently, in many ways the debate was quite one-sided.

Although the Anti-Federalists had a number of concerns, their single biggest concern was that the powerful new *federal* layer of government that had been created would ultimately evolve into tyranny. Consequently, they were adamant about the need for a bill of rights to help protect fundamental individual, inalienable rights against the kinds of government infringements they had experienced. The addition of a bill of rights to the Constitution was originally controversial because the Constitution, as written, did not specifically enumerate or protect the rights of the people. Rather, it listed the *limited* powers of the government and left all that remained to the states and the people. A majority of the Federalists, on the other hand, opposed any kind of bill of Rights. They argued that any such enumeration, once written down explicitly, could later be interpreted as a list of the only rights the people had. In response to this assertion, in so-called Anti-Federalist No. 84, "Brutus" argued that government unrestrained by such a bill could easily devolve into tyranny. Other supporters of the bill argued that a list of rights would not and should not be interpreted as exhaustive—that these rights were merely examples of important natural rights bestowed by their Creator that people had—but that other such natural rights existed as well, whether they were enumerated or not. People from this school of thought were confident that the judiciary would interpret these rights in an expansive fashion.

Although the Anti-Federalists were at a distinct disadvantage in their public relations campaigns, their efforts were not without effect. Ultimately, all thirteen of the original colonies voted to ratify the Constitution but only after a commitment was made to add a bill of rights. The

Bill of Rights, constituting the first ten amendments of the Constitution, were ratified effective December 15, 1791. As noted in the introductory material to *Bedrock!,* however, with the exception of the Bill of Rights, the Constitution was largely a product of the Federalist agenda.

Much has happened in the roughly 220 years since then. Our governments have *evolved.* The Civil War was a major turning point. The Great Depression was another. Finally, 9/11, the War on Terror, and the financial situation of the past few years have created new turning points that we need to understand and take into consideration as we move forward.

The Concept of *Federalism* Revisited and Clarified

In *Bedrock!* we talked at some length about the concept of *Federalism* and how little understood and confusing it is. At this point, it is time for some clarification. We even need to clarify and correct a few things we said in *Bedrock!*

Today, the average person typically associates the term *Federalism* with the federal government and therefore thinks that it represents the concept of *federal dominion* and a strong, centralized federal government. That is the practical definition we used in *Bedrock!* That was the practical understanding we and essentially everyone else in America grew up with. But historically in this country, even among the original Federalists, it meant just the opposite. Federalism was the concept of *divided* power. It was the opposite of *centralism* and consolidated power. It represented the concept of a federation—a union—of separate, individual, autonomous states acting together as a union of *united* states, with neither any individual state nor the union of states having dominion over any other states. The whole notion was based on the twin concepts of *division of power* and *balance* between and among competing entities.

Neither the Federalists nor the Anti-Federalists argued for an all powerful, centralized national government in which the states would be mere branches—subdivisions or departments of the larger federal government. The Anti-Federalists argued for states as completely separate, sovereign nations, loosely joined under an umbrella confederation (much like the Articles of Confederation). The Federalists, on the other hand, argued for two separate layers of government—one consisting of the states acting in their individual capacities and the other with the states acting together as a union of individual but united states. Even according to the Federalists' vision, this system was intended to have plenty of checks and balances and a healthy balance of power between the two layers of government. It was never intended that the federal layer would become so dominant or that Federalism, as applied, would come to mean what so many people think it means today—which is what makes the concept and its meaning so confusing.

Today, in many people's minds the applied concept or definition of Federalism has essentially evolved to mean the same as centralism, with essentially all power consolidated in Washington, D.C., and the federal government. Obviously, the roots of this evolution began even before—but blossomed following—the Civil War. Since then it has evolved steadily in one direction to the point that it has now reached full-bloom, centralized *federal dominion,* which is a completely different concept than Federalism.

The Original Federalist Agenda has Morphed into the Progressive Agenda

Although we have sought to avoid labels as much as possible in our discussions, at this point a few labels and their associated meanings and applications are again unavoidable. Because the popular concept of Federalism is now so confusing, both in terms of theory and how it has evolved in application, although centralism better describes what many people think of when they hear the term today, the popular label that now best describes how the original Federalist *agenda* has mutated and morphed over time and in application is *Progressivism.*

The original Federalist Agenda of Alexander Hamilton has now evolved, mutated and morphed into the Progressive Agenda. In a nutshell, the primary objective of the Progressive agenda is to consolidate and centralize power (does that sound like Alexander Hamilton and parts of his original Federalist vision?). It is a centralist vision—and not just at the national level in Washington, D.C. Ultimately the Progressive agenda advocates and strives for consolidation and centralization of *all* power. This agenda has no limitations, geographic or otherwise. And contrary to popular misconception, neither of the two major political parties has been immune to this agenda. In fact, both parties have fully embraced and been full participants in this agenda. But we're getting ahead of ourselves.

Fundamental Questions

At this point, we want people to ask and carefully consider the answer to some core questions: (1) "How do you feel about the path we're currently on?" (2) "Are we on the right path?" (3) "What is the destination going to look like when we get there?" As our good friend Worth Woolsey likes to say, "One of the big keys to happiness and success is not necessarily getting what you want but wanting what you get." Another big looming question is "Are we on track to want and like what we end up with?" Is it too early to tell, or do we have a pretty good idea already?

On one hand, compared with when the original Federalist / Anti-Federalist debate occurred, engaging in this discussion today is easier because of the broad spectrum of media outlets available for public discourse. On the other hand, finding an effective way to make one's voice heard above the din is a real challenge. The real question, though, is "How many people really even care?" As Worth says, "The vast majority of people really aren't interested in getting educated or involved. They just want to be stroked." We hope, however, that there *are* enough people who care, that they will seek to understand the realities of our situation and what needs to be done to fix it, and, most important, that they will be willing to stand up and do something about it to make a difference.

We believe this country is currently situated in such a way that time is of the essence. We know that this essay and our other essays are not perfect, either in form or content. Despite their imperfections, we know that the principles discussed will make a difference for good when applied. This work is a wake-up call and a call to action—a guide for taking stock of where we stand in the world today, for taking basic steps to strengthen the foundation of this great country, and for correcting course as necessary to achieve America's ultimate divine destiny.

We hope that our essays will be the functional equivalent of Paul Revere on his midnight rides, waking up the countryside, calling the colonists to action, and rallying the revolutionary patriots to battle for freedom and liberty and to fight against the tyranny and oppression.

We face similar challenges today. We need to wake up and start doing something about it—before it's too late.

Chapter 1

Where Governments Get Their Power and What They Do with It

In *Bedrock!* we discussed the basic laws of nature, both as they apply to individuals as well as to society collectively, including the basic natural laws that apply to governments. We begin this discussion focusing on the core principles that apply to government.

Basic Laws of Nature that Apply to Human Government

When a society puts a common government into effect, the laws of nature must be the guiding principles in order for that government to be successful in honoring the rights of the society, including the inalienable rights of individuals. The laws of nature, especially those pertaining to common government and the natural tendencies of those who govern, should be acknowledged and accommodated. Such natural laws include the following concepts:

- Personal responsibility, freedom of choice (liberty) and self-governance are the core foundational principles of government. Self-governance is the foundation of all government.

- Human beings should be entitled to govern themselves entirely and without interference unless their self-governance interferes with someone else's equal freedom of choice and right of self-governance.

Because history shows that self-governance is a challenge, however, common government becomes a necessity. Consequently, common government and resulting laws are instituted primarily for application to those situations where individuals fail to satisfactorily govern themselves.

Laws are instituted to deter actions that harm others and provide consequences for the violation of these and other laws.

- Common government and laws limiting self-governance should exist only by consent of those governed by such laws.

- The primary, paramount purpose of government is to protect inalienable, individual rights, including life, liberty, and the pursuit of happiness (property).

Those chosen to lead and govern others should be chosen by consent of the people to be governed. In cases where there is no unanimous consent, the majority determines who is to lead and govern (democratic republic).

Those chosen to lead and govern others are naturally obligated to act in the best interests of the people they are governing, subject to the laws of nature.

- When the best interests of people conflict, the interests of a majority of the people should be protected, subject to the laws of nature, including protection of individual inalienable rights. These rights should not be infringed upon regardless of what the majority may say or the size or strength of the majority (constitutionally limited republic).

- It is the natural disposition of almost all men, as they get authority, to begin to exercise unjust dominion. Power has a natural tendency to corrupt.

- When people are given power over others, their natural tendency is to begin to advance their own self-interests ahead of those of the governed and to exercise greater power and control than necessary, resulting in unjust dominion. And the longer they are in power, the more difficulty they have resisting these tendencies. Duration of power enhances the tendency toward corruption.

- The governed are entitled to know what their leaders are doing and to have input into the decisions their leaders make.

- Regardless of any man-made laws to the contrary, those chosen to lead and govern others are subject to applicable laws of nature and are directly accountable to those they govern.

- When human beings create government, they have an obligation to support the core functions of government, both financially, by exercising their right to vote, and through service. The resulting government is likewise obligated to protect, defend, and preserve fundamental individual rights, including life, liberty, and property.

- Government that governs least governs best.

Natural Results and Cycles of Governments Based on the Laws of Nature

What follows is a list of self-evident truths based on the lessons of history respecting the establishment, continuation, natural consequences, sequences, and cycles of human governments:

- According to the laws of nature, human governments can be established in only one of two ways: by force, resulting from lack of consent; or by mutual consent, resulting from the exercise of freedom of choice (liberty) by those to be governed.

- Likewise, once established, governments continue to exist only by force or the continued consent of the governed.

- Lasting freedom, peace, and prosperity exist in societies where governments generally adhere to the laws of nature; govern with the consent of the governed; protect individual, inalienable rights; and peacefully transfer power in accordance with the rule of law.

- History reveals the self-evident truth that no human government has been perpetuated indefinitely.

- Once government leaders acquire power, by whatever means, they have a natural tendency to protect their own self-interests, control others, and inevitably desire to exercise more power and control than is necessary. This results in unjust dominion, which inevitably violates the laws of nature and infringes on (abuses) individual, inalienable rights.

- When a government exercises unjust dominion or infringes upon individual inalienable rights, the stability once provided by that government weakens, the consent of the governed is eventually withdrawn, and the only way government can continue to govern is by force.

- If a government continually violates the laws of nature and abuses inalienable, individual rights to the point that a large enough group is no longer willing to tolerate such abuses, the people eventually withdraw their consent to be governed by the government. They then seek to either overthrow the government by force or replace it with a less-abusive government.

- Once mutual consent to be governed is withdrawn, the only way a government can continue to govern is by force.

- As a general rule, human governments end in one or more of the following ways, which involve either force or withdrawal of consent by the governed:

1. Coup d'état (typically by the military or with military backing)
2. Revolution (violent or peaceful)
3. Civil war
4. Attack and overthrow by outside forces
5. Stagnation, deterioration, and collapse from within
6. Peaceful transition and replacement with a new form of government

The more or longer a government exercises unjust dominion, violates and acts inconsistently with the laws of nature, and infringes upon inalienable individual rights, the more likely and more quickly its demise—unless its continuation and perpetuation is maintained by forceful means.

In the absence of ordered government, law-of-the-jungle anarchy prevails until someone internally or externally exercises control by force or by mutual consent.

"I'M GETTING TIRED OF HUNTING AND GATHERING. LET'S INVENT TAXES AND GOVERNMENT."

Chapter 2

Proper Roles and Structure of Government

With a basic understanding of the laws of nature that apply to government, before we can begin the work of fixing the foundation, and correcting course, a concept we need to be very clear on is proper roles, particularly with respect to government. Here in America, much confusion exists about the roles government is meant to play. Whether because of government overstepping its bounds or because of people lacking understanding, most of us are unsure of what makes good sense in accordance with the laws of nature when it comes to the proper roles government should be playing.

Core Principles

Contrary to common belief, the Constitution is not the foundation of our country, our society, or our civilization. Instead, the laws of nature and nature's God are the bedrock, and *"We the People of the United States,"* together with this patch of earth and the resources it contains, are the foundation. The Constitution is the structural foundation of our federal government, and it serves as the core structure for our governmental relationships, which are built on the foundation of we the people. But in reality, constitutional principles are just tools we use to effectively utilize the bedrock. The Constitution is intended to be the foundational tool we use in helping us recognize and adhere to the laws of nature. The Preamble to the Constitution can help us understand this:

"We the People of the United States, in Order to form a more perfect Union, establish Justice, insure domestic Tranquility, provide for the common defense, promote the general Welfare, and secure the Blessings of Liberty to ourselves and our Posterity, do ordain and establish this Constitution for the United States of America."

The Declaration of Independence, after making specific reference to the "Laws of Nature and of Nature's God" and the "unalienable Rights" endowed by the Creator, including life, liberty, and the pursuit of happiness, avers:

"Governments are instituted among Men, deriving their just powers from the consent of the governed . . . [but] whenever any Form of Government becomes destructive of these ends, it is the Right of the People to alter or to abolish it, and to institute new Government, laying its foundation on such principles and organizing its powers in such form, as to them shall seem most likely to effect their Safety and Happiness. Prudence, indeed, will dictate, that Governments long established should not be changed for light and transient causes; and accordingly all experience hath shewn, that mankind are more disposed to suffer, while evils are sufferable, than to right themselves by abolishing the forms to which they are accustomed. But when a long train of abuses and usurpations, pursuing invariably the same Object evinces a design to reduce them under absolute Despotism, it is their right, it is their duty, to throw off such Government, and to provide new Guards for their future security."

The Fundamental Concept of Personal Responsibility

To effectively apply these words to our current situation, we must clearly understand at least basic, core principles of the laws of nature and the foundational concept of personal responsibility. That understanding will help us better grasp the proper roles of individuals, families, communities, churches, charities, business, media, and so forth. As people and entities take responsibility for their proper roles in accordance with the laws of nature, the role of government—specifically the federal government—becomes more limited and organically falls into its proper place.

One incorrect notion that must be corrected is that it is not the job of government to save people from the natural consequences of their decisions and actions. Rather, under our Constitution, the paramount role of government is to defend, protect, and preserve the fundamental inalienable rights of life, liberty, and property. Secondary priorities include the preservation of safety and security as well as *general* welfare and stability, but not in opposition to fundamental individual rights. With the Tenth Amendment, our Founding Fathers sought to clarify the limited role they intended the federal government to play.

Maintaining Neutrality with Respect to Private Enterprise

Governments and elected officials in this country—at all levels—have gotten in the bad habit of feeling that it is their place to choose sides and attempt to pick winners and losers in private enterprise. A situation that we have chosen to use as an ongoing example for discussion of principles in a number of different contexts throughout this essay is the recent controversy over the so-called "Ground Zero Mosque" in New York City. The controversy surrounds the proposed construction of an Islamic center approximately two city blocks from Ground Zero, the former site of the twin towers of the World Trade Center, which collapsed after being attacked on 9/11, killing thousands of people trapped inside the buildings. Among other things, it has been widely publicized, for example, that New York City mayor Michael Bloomberg and other politicians favor or disfavor construction of this center. The fundamental question is why do our government leaders feel compelled to take such positions and make such pronouncements, as if it were their place to do so? Why do government leaders feel compelled to pick sides in private enterprise and promote the agendas of special interests in an obvious attempt to influence who wins and who loses? Why do they have to be for or against such ventures? Why not just govern by taking a neutral, objective position, applying fundamental principles uniformly and making decisions based on applicable criteria in accordance with the rule of law rather than based on slanted agendas?

The Fundamental Hierarchy of Government

All governmental tasks and functions should be undertaken at the lowest possible level of government. Tax dollars are best collected and spent at a local level. It is at the local level that more accountability can be brought to bear and that less waste and fraud in government bureaucracy will be tolerated. If a task is better handled on a higher level, it can be moved up the ladder as needed. The states of this republic created the federal government to take responsibility for performing certain limited and well-defined tasks, such as providing for a national defense and conducting international relations. These were tasks the states could not reasonably perform on their own but from which they all would equally benefit.

It was not the federal government that created the states but the states that created the federal government. Hence, the federal government, when performing its appropriate role, does not have the right to dictate law or procedure to the states or to usurp the proper roles of state and local governments.

Essential Local Government Functions and Services

The core role of local government pertains to the general health, safety, and welfare of its community. Unlike the specific, limited, and enumerated powers delegated to the federal government, local governments have a general mandate and can be more expansive or flexible as the people decide what is needed in individual communities.

Local governments often properly take responsibility for certain essential services, such as fire protection and emergency response as well as providing drinking water, wastewater treatment, and garbage disposal. Local governments may also coordinate the provision of other utilities and essential services. None of these functions need be provided by the government itself; they can be provided by the private sector or by other government providers. But these are all appropriate functions of local government as dictated and supported by citizens of the community.

Certain local government responsibilities, however, cannot reasonably be delegated to the private sector. These include law enforcement, administration of justice, and coordination of land uses. Even in these areas, local government must maintain a limited role and accountability to the people. There should be checks and balances to deter personal agendas or corrupt partnerships. Local governments must recognize, for example, that people have fundamental inalienable property rights and are entitled to exercise their fundamental liberties to use their property as they wish, as long as such use does not substantially interfere with public health, safety, and welfare. Unfortunately, this is an area where many local governments have become just as abusive of inalienable, individual rights as any other level of government.

Again, we turn to the so-called "Ground Zero Mosque," not so much to get caught up in that particular issue, but to use it as a familiar and fitting example and context for discussion and application of fundamental principles, illustrating how such principles apply to real issues and situations that arise. Inevitably, some will disagree with our position, but the mosque is a prime example of how people want government at all levels to intervene to do things that violate private property rights. In this case, the primary stated justification for attempting to block construction of the mosque is insensitivity to the victims of 9/11.

We fully acknowledge these sensitivities, including the fact that Ground Zero is considered hallowed ground. Not only did a large number of Americans tragically die there, but it is also the final resting place of some of those people. Based on such sensitivities, the solution some might offer would be to create yet another layer of governmental property regulation, including something like a "Ground Zero Overlay Zone" that defines an area around Ground Zero and places additional restrictions on what can be done with property within that zone. While we can understand the temptation to consider doing something like that, regardless of the sensitivities and how we may feel about mosques or the people who worship in them, since when does attempting to mediate such insensitivities have anything to do with government's paramount role of protecting inalienable, individual rights, including life, liberty, and property?

Only a handful of inalienable, individual rights bestowed by our Creator are among the laws of nature and nature's God expressly listed and protected by the Constitution, including freedom of expression and the right to worship. Such rights also expressly include liberty—freedom of choice as well as fundamental private property rights. But as far as we can tell, natural rights against the insensitivity of others, just like purported rights to affordable health care, quality housing, quality public education, and corporate free speech, do not exist among the natural rights bestowed by our Creator. So where do we get the idea that such unnatural notions should be entitled to governmental and constitutional protection?

There are fundamental universal principles of government that transcend time, location, and current events. In accordance with the laws of nature and nature's God, our Constitution, and the rule of law, the paramount role of governments, including the governing bodies in Lower Manhattan, should be protection of life, liberty, and property. When circumstances occur where mediation of sensitivities is at odds with protection of such fundamental inalienable rights, protection of those rights must be the highest priority, regardless of how we may feel or how hard the winds of the media or public opinion may blow.

Unfortunately, many local governments and local government leaders have been brainwashed into forgetting and disregarding the fundamental laws of nature, particularly with respect to property rights. These governments and leaders have somehow been persuaded to adopt restrictive zoning laws and pass cookie-cutter land-use ordinances that completely ignore inalienable property rights bestowed by the laws of nature. Such entities and individuals themselves pretend to be the source of all property rights and entitlements.

Many times their ordinances elevate form over substance, placing the vast majority of their emphasis on aesthetics and other superficial values at the expense of fundamental substantive values like production. And they completely ignore that the single, highest priority and role of government—at every level—is to protect and preserve individual, inalienable rights, including fundamental property rights. Because of this, many local governments have attempted to enact and enforce private contract-like land-use regulations that egregiously violate individual rights. Except for *coordination,* local governments need to stay out of the way rather than get right in the way and create roadblocks they force everyone to navigate around as they pick and choose those they wish to help pilot through the mess.

While any such actions should be measured against these standards, limited terms and expansive citizen involvement can also help provide the counterbalance that keeps such decisions out of the hands of a few officials and in the control of the neighborhoods that the decisions affect most.

Proper Role of Counties, Burroughs, and Functional Equivalents

County governments should function in many respects much as municipalities. Their responsibility is mostly for unincorporated areas outside municipal boundaries but within county jurisdiction. In those places, it is a county's role to provide basic government services, including law enforcement and a justice system. As the U.S. Supreme Court held in *Printz v. United States,* the federal government has no authority to tell state and local officials what to do, and state, county, and local officials are not obligated to enforce federal laws. In any county, the officials elected by residents of that county have as much or more authority than the president of the United States in those local jurisdictions.

Counties also possess coordinating functions that cover both the unincorporated areas as well as all municipalities within their boundaries, along with the responsibility to collect and distribute property taxes. Counties also provide some organizational functions for all within the county, such as the recorder's office, where all real estate transactions in the county, including within municipal boundaries, are recorded.

As services and functions are retained at the lowest possible governmental level, the people maintain greater control over their own lives and the services that affect them. There are some coordinating functions that can be better accomplished by a county, acting as an umbrella entity, than by a municipality. But counties should never attempt to usurp any municipal powers.

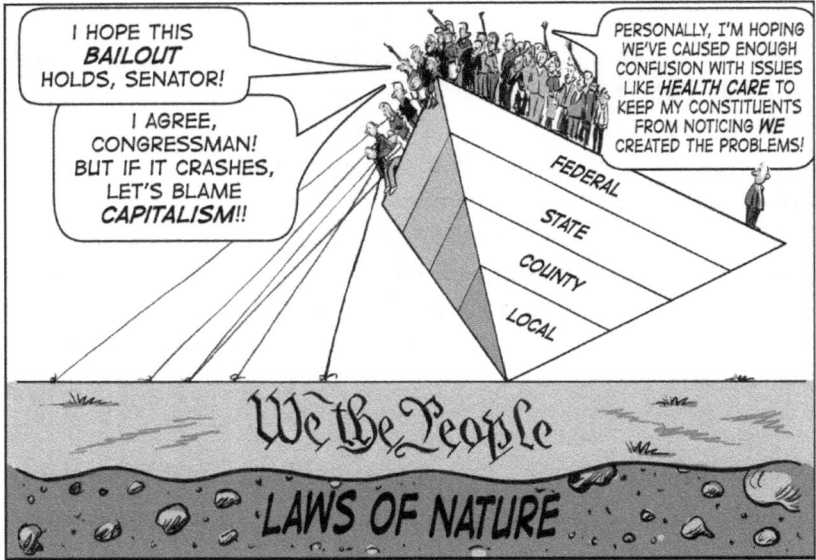

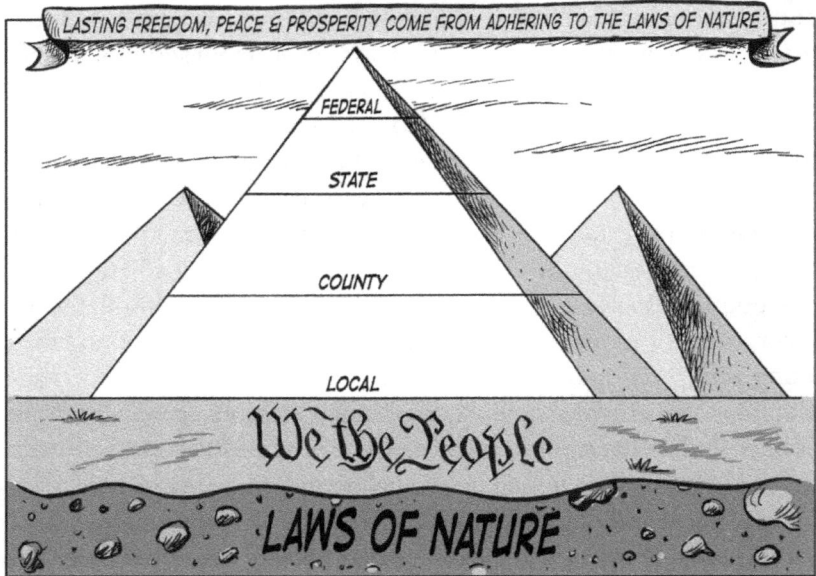

Proper Role of State Governments

On balance, the proper role of state governments should be considerably more limited than that of local and county governments. There are, however, a few things that local governments simply can't handle, so these naturally fall to the states. These functions include coordinated public safety and administration of justice as well as statewide transportation coordination, planning, construction, and maintenance. States are also in a better position to engage in natural resource and environmental regulation. Some tax revenue, such as funds for roads and funds from sales tax, are best collected at the state level and distributed to local governments. States also have an important role in public safety and protection through state police and the National Guard. States also set the rules under which their political subdivisions (towns, cites, service districts, and counties) operate, and they are responsible to see that local entities act through a system of constitutional checks and balances.

Proper Role of the Federal Government

The proper role of the federal government is pretty small. Spelled out in Article 1, Section 8, of the U.S. Constitution, the list includes national defense (security), international and interstate commerce, naturalization, coinage of money, postal services, and some administration of justice, including resolution of disputes among the states. *The Tenth Amendment clarifies that all other powers are reserved to the states and we the people.*

The proper role of the federal government—acting as a union of the states—is limited to those things that we the people and the states, individually, are not well situated to do. Unfortunately, the federal government has completely disregarded the Tenth Amendment and has effectively sought to usurp a vast array of governmental roles, including primary responsibility for general health, safety, and welfare. In the process, the federal government has made the states and us its slaves.

Although the Supremacy Clause (Article VI, Section 2) is often waved as a Federalist and progressive banner that purportedly justifies anything the federal government wants to do, under the Constitution the federal government properly has supremacy only in those detailed, limited areas where it has been granted specific authority and jurisdiction. Among those, the Commerce Clause has now been interpreted broadly enough to include everything, including the kitchen sink, as interstate commerce. In the federal government tool kit, the Commerce Clause and the Supremacy Clause have become twin hammers that are the first tools the federal government uses to intervene in virtually every circumstance. It is highly doubtful that our federalist forefathers could have foreseen that the federal government would ultimately abandon the regular and appropriate use of most of the other tools at its disposal in favor of using these twin hammers to bludgeon almost every situation into federal submission.

Considerable confusion exists with regard to the proper roles of the respective branches of the federal government. According to the Constitution, it is the proper role of the legislative branch of government (Congress) to make laws—all laws. It is the proper role of the judicial branch to interpret and apply the laws. And it is the proper role of the executive branch to execute, or enforce, the laws. Today, all three branches seek to make law, all three branches seek to interpret and apply the law, and all three branches seek to enforce the law. In the process, the original system of checks and balances has been grievously compromised. In no case is this more manifest than with the fourth, or administrative, branch of the federal government—a branch that has no constitutional basis.

Is Social Security within the proper constitutional role of the federal government? No. Nor is Medicaid, Medicare, or the Patient Protection and Affordable Care Act (PPACA), the newest healthcare act. We need good stewardship of our natural resources, but the Environmental Protection Agency (EPA), the Forest Service, and the Bureau of Land Management (BLM) should not exist as federal entities. The Federal Reserve? No. FEMA? No. The USDA, SEC, FDA, OSHA, INS, ATF, IRS, HUD? No. The list of government administrations that exist outside the proper limits of the federal government is practically endless. In any reform of governmental roles, it is the fourth, or administrative, branch that needs most to be reined in, brought to heel, and made accountable to the people through the states and within the authoritative framework outlined in the Constitution.

Discretionary, *social program* functions virtually all fall outside the proper role of government—specifically the federal government. They also generally violate the fundamental laws of nature. At lower levels of government where health, safety, and welfare mandates do have a place, such programs should only exist when the general public gives its consent. Likewise, all taxes collected for those purposes should be collected and spent at the lowest level possible, giving the people better access to government, more say as to what these programs should cost, and how resources should be utilized.

Separation of Powers and Checks and Balances

In any theoretical discussion of the Constitution and government in this country, say in a high school civics class or in a college political science course, there is always much discussion about separation of powers, balance of power, and checks and balances. We hear much about checks and balances in our system of government, but the looming questions are "Where is the balance between the federal government and the states?" and "What checks are there on the federal government?" At this point, the answer is that there is no balance. There are no checks on federal power. Rather, the federal government is continually *checking* the states and trying to tell them what they can and can't do. But there is no corresponding *check* on the federal government.

Our government has evolved to the point that there is little separation of powers in the relationship between the federal government and the states. The federal government essentially treats the states as if they were simply one more cog in the federal machine, one step down from federal agencies. And unfortunately, many states have come to view themselves the same way, looking to the federal government both for direction and resources to operate. In the process, they have become highly dependent. The states were always intended to have a balancing effect on the federal government. But in losing the separation of powers, all balance has likewise been lost. The federal government has become a law unto itself with no accountability. It operates completely unchecked, with no accountability to anyone, including the states, or we the people.

Other Roles in Our Society

In *Prosperity!* we touch briefly on the proper roles of private sector entities, including individuals, families, churches, charities, private sector business generally, and the media. The only one of those entities we are going to address here is the media.

There was a time in American history when the media—then known as "the Press"—was sometimes referred to as the "fourth branch of government"—the transparency and accountability branch—and lauded for its *objective* role in reporting the news and holding government at all levels accountable for its actions. That is hardly the case today. Instead, the mainstream media has essentially jumped on the bandwagon and become one of the primary tools of government—especially the federal government. In today's world, the mainstream media has become a spin doctor, often doing the government's bidding, but otherwise most loyal to its own agenda, and point of view, with little actual regard for the masses it is pretending to "keep informed." In many cases, that agenda resembles the same progressive agenda that seems to have consumed both political parties as well as this country and its governments.

Again, the controversy over the Ground Zero Mosque is a good example of the kind of spin the media puts on things to promote its agenda. In that case, an accurate and objective statement would include a precise description of the proposed development and would state that it would be located approximately two blocks from Ground Zero. Such a statement might also note that there are already other mosques in the same area. But someone in the media created an entirely new buzz phrase when they began calling it the "Ground Zero Mosque," and everyone else piled on, making it sound as though it were right next door or across the street and that its proposed construction was the epitome of insensitivity to the victims of 9/11. Using this deceptive spin to its advantage, the media and others have stirred up a national frenzy about the mosque, seeking to get everyone from the president to a wide variety of other prominent public figures to weigh in on the subject. At this point, rather than having any clear stake in the final outcome, it appears the media's primary objective was just to stir up controversy.

This is nonsense. First of all, the situation should be fairly and objectively reported. Second, attempting to stir controversy and make a federal case of it is wrong. Despite what happened at ground zero, decisions about what to do with the proposed development are local issues for local government to resolve based on solid governmental principles without being blown all over the map by the windy mainstream media and what everyone else in this country thinks. The issue should be resolved by the governing bodies in Lower Manhattan based on fundamental principles and the rule of law, which should govern their decisions. Although everyone else is certainly entitled to have and express an opinion—and such discussion and debate is healthy—we should not be misled by the media to believe that everyone else has any genuine stake or standing in the matter or say in the decision.

If more people really understood who should be involved in making the decision and what the true and legitimate basis for the decision should be, maybe everyone else would be more inclined to mind their own business. But the media has come to operate and act as though it has a legitimate and personal stake (to stir up controversy) as well as a philosophical agenda in just about everything that happens, and it does its best to promote that agenda.

Chapter 3

What We Have Done with Government in America

Before turning our attention to discussion of specific steps that can and need to be taken to address these issues, we need to more fully examine some other core issues as they relate to our governments and how they fulfill their roles. Although the laws of nature are at the root of the dialogue, what else is fundamentally wrong with this country? In that regard, we're going to cut right to the chase.

We have Replaced God with BIG Government

In *Bedrock!*, we described the core, bedrock foundation of our existence, and *it is not government.* In that discussion, we attempted to take a fairly soft approach to this whole issue, attempting to provide milk as food for thought before putting the meat on the table. To that end, we soft-pedaled this issue to some extent, couching it primarily in terms of the "laws of nature." But as clearly articulated in the Declaration of Independence, the laws of nature are also the laws of nature's God—that great Creator of heaven and earth by whom all mankind are created as equals and endowed with certain inalienable rights, including life, liberty, and the pursuit of happiness. According to the Declaration of Independence, "[It is only] to secure these rights, [that] Governments are created among Men, deriving their just powers from the consent of the governed." In other words, government is not intended to be the *end* but should be viewed and used rather as a means to the end.

Consequently, the core foundation and bedrock of our existence includes not only the laws of nature but also the laws of nature's God, which are actually one and the same. Both the Creator—God—and all divine creations are part of that foundation, that bedrock of our existence. Government is just an unnatural, man-made tool that we the people have created for the express purpose of assisting us in securing and protecting inalienable God-given rights. Yet we have attempted to replace the bedrock with that tool, attempting to make government not just a means to an end but the end itself—a new, artificial, counterfeit foundation for our existence.

In the process, we have not only allowed government to take over, but we have also lost both our faith and our moral compass. In fact, loss of our faith and moral compass is why we have allowed government to take over. Instead of continuing to turn to God, we turned to government to the point that now, to a large extent, government has replaced God in our collective lives. And we have likewise done everything in our power to remove God from government.

Separation of Church and State

Undoubtedly, one of the reasons for the big push to remove God from all government is a vast misunderstanding and misinterpretation of the Establishment Clause of the First Amendment to the Constitution. The First Amendment states, "Congress shall make no law respecting an establishment of religion, or prohibiting the free exercise thereof." This law expressly applies to Congress, but like the Supremacy Clause and the Commerce Clause, it has been interpreted so broadly that courts in this country have now held that it applies to every level of government. Virtually any act that could possibly be conceived as having any religious significance is viewed as a prohibited "establishment of religion." Although the U.S. Supreme Court and supreme court justices have opined on the subject, obviously they don't get it.

Acknowledgment of and recognition that God exists is not an establishment of religion. Yet courts in this country, including the Supreme Court with a so-called *conservative* majority, have pursued this path of removing God from government with the same kind of vigor they have used in relying on the Supremacy Clause and the Commerce Clause to pursue a progressive agenda advocated by both major political parties.

As opposed to how it has been interpreted and applied, the fundamental purpose of the Establishment Clause was to prevent the federal government from establishing a state religion or applying force when it comes to religion, as had been done throughout the ages in Europe and elsewhere. But that objective has morphed well beyond the original intent. It is now used as one of the primary tools for replacing God with godlessness—including in government. We have lost our fundamental understanding of liberty when it comes to the concept of faith, God, and religion. We have lost our fundamental concept of liberty in general. Liberty means freedom of choice. Liberty creates options. When those options are taken away, we are deprived of liberty. It is amazing how on one hand our governments are now so hypersensitive and defensive about any possible religious themes, while on the other hand they are so quick to apply force in many other areas (as discussed in more detail later).

All of this, including everything we have allowed our governments to do, reflects our morals, values, and priorities as a people and as a society. If we want a godless government and nation, our elected leaders and judges have done their best to give us what we want. If we want something else, it's up to us to understand and do what is required to make it happen.

"Hey, don't look at me — I was *against* free will."

Chapter 4

Government Has Gotten Out of Control

Contrary to many of the assertions made by the authors of the *Federalist Papers*, primarily including Alexander Hamilton, two hundred years of experience has taught us that government, by its very nature, is greedy and can't seem to help or stop itself. Who can sincerely argue that government in this nation, especially the federal government, has not become exactly what the Anti-Federalists feared it would become? As in the following tale, we should have recognized these natural propensities from the start.

The Little Boy and the Rattlesnake

A little boy was out for a walk and encountered a rattlesnake. The rattlesnake was old, so he asked, "Please, little boy, can you take me to the top of the mountain? I hope to see the sunset one last time before I die."

The little boy answered, "No, Mr. Rattlesnake. If I pick you up, you'll bite me and I'll die."

The rattlesnake said, "No, I promise I won't bite you. Just please take me up to the mountain."

The little boy thought for a moment. Then he picked up the rattlesnake and held it close to his chest as he carried it to the top of the mountain. They sat and watched the beautiful sunset together. Then the rattlesnake turned to the boy and asked, "Please, little boy, will you take me back to my home now? I am tired and I am old. It is time for me to leave this world, and I would like to return to my home now."

The little boy thought for a moment. He had been safe all this time and the snake had kept its word, so the boy decided to take it home. He carefully picked up the snake again, held it close to his chest, and carried it back down the mountain.

Just before the boy laid it down, the rattlesnake turned and bit him in the chest. "Mr. Rattlesnake," the boy cried out as he threw the snake on the ground, "why did you do that? Now I will die!"

The rattlesnake looked at him and said, "You knew what I was when you picked me up."

We the People Are the Parents and Grandparents

Just as we must recognize the snake for who he is, it is also imperative that we remember who we are. We must realize and remember that we the people created our governments. The power resides with us. We are the parents, so to speak, of our governments. As the supreme power, we the people, acting through states, created the federal government. The states, then, are our children and are equal siblings in the American family, while the federal government is the sole grandchild and is directly accountable to us as the parents and grandparents.

Unfortunately, neither state nor federal governments demonstrate much accountability. What we now have on our hands is a federal government that acts like a spoiled three-year-old running the house—or worse, what was a spoiled three-year-old now grown up to be a belligerent teenager or young adult with no respect for his parents or grandparents.

Do you remember the fable in *Bedrock!* about the camel that wanted to stick its nose inside the tent during the sandstorm? The federal government is the epitome of that camel. Over the last two centuries, it has

inched its way into our lives until there is no longer any room (or control) left for us. We the people are getting pushed out of our tent and into the storm while the camel rests comfortably inside.

The New Fourth Branch of Government

As we mentioned earlier, there was a time when the press was sometimes referred to as the fourth branch of government because of its role in holding the government accountable for its actions. That is hardly the case today. In fact, for the most part, the mainstream media has largely abdicated this role; its main objective now seems to be to provide support for the government's agenda—especially the federal government.

The new fourth branch of government is the administrative branch. This regulatory branch was never conceived of by our Founding Fathers and never authorized in the Constitution, yet it is ceaseless in its hunger for more power and control. The administrative branch is the federal government's slave master and has grown to dwarf all other branches of the government combined. It consumes the vast majority of the federal budget, with expenditures in the trillions. This branch of government is notoriously inept at managing its resources, and it produces nothing. It only consumes. It is like a great parasite living on our nation.

Although we the people have elected representatives, we have never authorized those representatives or the executive branch to do the things they are doing. The Constitution makes no provision for the majority of the laws and regulations put in place by this administrative branch of government, yet they have increasing power over our lives. This is due in part to the little-understood differences between a constitutional republic and a mob-rule democracy. Decades ago, a majority in Congress and the executive branch decided that they wanted to create a new branch of government, so they did. The power of this entity has grown by leaps and bounds since then, and we the people have been steadily edged out without ever realizing we should have stopped it.

This fourth branch of government resembles a massive *McMansion* addition to a tidy, well-built house. Our original house was built solidly on a strong foundation (the power of the people) with a sturdy core structure of floors, walls, beams, and trusses (the Constitution). The McMansion monstrosity (administrative government) is a flimsy yet oversized add-on, shoddily built on a thin slab of uncompacted sand, completely removed from the bedrock of the laws of nature and the foundation of power derived from the people. In addition to being illicitly constructed, it is ugly, overwhelming, and crippling to the original structure.

Included in this fourth branch are many regulatory agencies never authorized by the Constitution. These regulatory agencies and the unelected administrators and *czars* who run them make the vast majority of laws, rules, and regulations that govern our lives. The current trend, in fact, is for legislative bodies to simply pass their initiatives off to one or more administrative regulatory agencies any time they run into a substantial hurdle in passing legislation backed by the party in power. The assigned agency then implements the agenda through an avalanche of new administrative rules and regulations. The number of *administrative* laws now vastly exceeds real laws made by elected lawmakers. The federal government is continually collaborating with the private sector, and when they can't accomplish their goals out in the open, they do it through this fourth branch of the government.

One example of this is the current administration's push for carbon cap-and-trade regulations, which would establish standards for capping carbon and other emissions and issue *carbon credits* that could be traded and exchanged in the market place through the EPA. When it appeared that cap-and-trade legislation would not pass both houses of Congress, it was handed off to the EPA to implement through administrative policies and regulations.

In addition to the underhanded implementation of new policies, the administrative branch has developed thousands of ineffective, parasitic agencies and programs that suck the financial resources out of our government coffers and the lifeblood out of our businesses, families, and people. Most of these programs are unbelievably complicated and seldom truly benefit the people intended. Many of the heavy-handed governmental abuses described later in the next chapter have come at the hands of the administrative branch—an illegitimate branch that was never meant to be.

Two hundred years after the creation of the Constitution, we have a federal government that is out of control—operating without checks and balances, with little accountability, and with a fourth branch running rogue (not to mention the inefficient practice of having virtually every agency duplicated at both the state and federal level). This results in power struggles, confusion, red tape, and an obscene waste of resources.

As has been pointed out by others, thanks to the establishment of this fourth branch of government, we now have a government of acronyms: the EPA, FCC, FSA, OSHA, MSHA, FEMA, FDA, FBI, CIA, INS, BATFE, HUD, BIA, SEC, DEA, CPS, BLM, DOE, and our own American version of the notorious Gestapo, the IRS. All of these agencies are members of an administrative conglomeration that was never meant to be yet controls our lives, our lands, our water, our crops, our guns, our air, our bodies, and our children.

Is this the alternative to oppressive British rule that our Founding Fathers envisioned would secure abundant lives, liberty, and opportunity to achieve happiness? As someone once wrote, "No, the thought makes reason stare."

It is a scientific certainty that the bigger government becomes, the more freedom shrinks—and at exactly the same pace. Our founders devised our government with only a few discreet and specifically enumerated powers precisely to discourage it from becoming the overwhelming, overregulating presence it is today. The attitude of our government has become that of a benevolent dictator. Its message is "We will do whatever it takes to feed you, clothe you, care for you, educate you, and protect you from yourself." In return, the government asks for our complete submission and compliance, and much of our resources. Instead of a government based on principles of personal choice, individual accountability, and self-determination, we have bonds of false security.

Mob-Rule Democracy Versus a Constitutional Republic

Few citizens understand that a democracy and a constitutional republic are not the same. Somewhere along the way, we the people of the United States have been hoodwinked into believing that our Founding Fathers wrote a constitution in order to establish a democracy. This is a gigantic error. Not even the Federalists argued for the establishment of a democracy. In reality, pure democracy—the will of the majority—is little more than mob rule. According to Benjamin Franklin "Democracy is two wolves and a lamb voting on what to have for lunch. Liberty is a well-armed lamb contesting the vote."

Democracy does not take into account fundamental inalienable, individual rights based on the laws of nature, which cannot and should not be infringed upon, no matter how big the majority. Truth is not determined by majority vote. The Constitution was written to ensure that basic fundamental rights are not violated, no matter what the majority may say.

The word *Democracy* is not written in any of our foundational documents. There had already been plenty of failed democracies throughout history by the time our nation was formed. It was not the intent of our Founding Fathers to put their lives at risk to start another one. The blood, sweat, tears, and sacrifice of fortunes that followed the signing of the Declaration of Independence and the writing and implementation of the Constitution were all about a new experiment—the experiment of a unique form of government based on the idea that "all men are created equal" and should be left to govern themselves. It was the intent of the Founders that the people retain an inviolable sovereignty and power over a government that was created to serve them—not vice versa—and that fundamental inalienable rights remain sacrosanct no matter what.

Exhaustive and strenuous effort went into the development of a system that would guarantee that those serving in government—especially those serving at the federal level—would not violate the rights of the citizens.

This was the first time in history that the norms of governance would be changed. Rulers had always governed people. Now, in America, the rulers themselves were to be governed *by* the people. The system was supposed to be replete with checks and balances so as to provide protections, keeping government off the backs of people and guaranteeing individual rights. The absolute and most vital of all rights to be protected was liberty, or, freedom of choice.

It is essential to understand that the intention of the Founding Fathers, even the most ardent Federalists, was to create a constitutional republic. This representative form of government, with its extremely limited powers, was to be confined within the parameters as expressly set forth by the supreme law of the land: the Constitution itself. It was intended that the Constitution be used to hold all levels and branches of government accountable to the people and to create inviolable protections for inalienable, individual rights, including life, liberty, and property.

It is important to understand the critical differences between a constitutional republic and a mob-rule democracy. In a pure democracy, everyone votes and the majority rules. Period. With this pack mentality, if the majority votes to have Larry for lunch, they do. There's nothing to stop that. There's no protection against tyranny of the majority in a democracy. Our Pilgrim ancestors tried pure democracy. They also tried having everything in common. Both systems proved unsuccessful. Pure democracy was extremely inefficient, and the community failed to thrive. But most important, there was nothing to stop the majority from violating the inalienable rights of individuals—which the majority did in some instances. Remember the Salem witch hunts? It wasn't until the people changed to a representative form of government and embraced the concept of private property that the community began to prosper, individually and collectively. Even more important, history has proven that constitutional protections are necessary to preserve inalienable individual rights against tyranny of the majority.

Slippery Slope

Under the constitutional republic form of government established by our Founding Fathers, regardless of majority opinion to the contrary, inalienable rights would not be subject to infringement. Moreover, this also applied to the states, which were intended to maintain both separation, and a degree of sovereignty and independence, preventing either the federal government or a majority of the other states from imposing their will on individual or even a minority of the states.

Much of that changed during the Civil War and the debate over slavery. That debate resulted from some unfinished business left over from the language of the Declaration of Independence and the Constitutional Convention. In earlier discussions related to those documents, considerable debate revolved around use of the phrase "pursuit of happiness" rather than "property" (which the phrase "pursuit of happiness" is generally interpreted to mean). In the end, the Founders reached an impasse regarding use of the word "property" because in some states at the time, the practical definition of that word included black slaves. Many of the Founders did not want the right to own slaves to be considered an inherent, inalienable right. They hoped that in time slavery would be undone on a state-by-state basis, and they did not want to create an obstacle in that corrective process. Ultimately, they settled on the phrase "pursuit of happiness" to avoid an endless and irresolvable debate over slavery at the time.

What most people do not realize today is that in order to correct the injustices of slavery, the president, Congress, and the federal government grossly exceeded their constitutional bounds during the Civil War. This fact has largely been swept under the rug. The rationale has always been that the end justified the means. Because slavery and the treatment of human beings were at issue, the government justified the bending of constitutional rules, and it still does—under the guise of something being best for the common good. But regardless of how just the cause, much of what was done by the federal government at that time was done outside of constitutional bounds. And what was done set an unlawful precedent that has been followed ever since. Today the federal government has completely forgotten that it is subject to constitutional limitations, and most people honestly believe that whatever the majority wants, goes. The way most citizens understand our government is that if most states want to tell North Dakota, for example, what it must do, they are entitled to do so.

How does such a government work in reality? In what ways is it actually applied? The list is long, but programs such as No Child Left Behind, mandatory health insurance, gun control, regulated property rights, federal environmental regulation, and immigration provide just a few examples.

Federal administrative regulations as well as direct acts of Congress usurp states' and individuals' rights and assume control. If, for example, the state of Wyoming says it wants to be responsible for managing its own natural resources, including wildlife and gray wolf populations within the state, it is no matter. Both Congress and other states believe they should be able to dictate, among other things, what Wyoming does and how such wolf populations are managed. Acting through Congress and the federal government, a majority of representatives from the rest of the states—who have little knowledge and no real stake in what happens in Wyoming—insist that they can tell Wyoming what to do with respect to gray wolves in the state.

A recent MSNBC article further illustrates this issue. The subject of the article was how Montana highway laws, including drunk driving and speeding laws, are evolving. According to the article, "Until 2005, when [Montana] came *under heavy duress* from the federal government, it was legal to drink and drive in many places. And a few years before that there wasn't even a speed limit on major highways and in rural areas."

While we adamantly oppose drinking and driving and certainly commend the Montana Legislature for addressing these issues, we hope it is doing so of its own volition and on its own terms without buckling and kowtowing to federal government pressure. We don't believe it's a federal issue. Why should the federal government be applying heavy duress to any state? That is like children disrespecting and applying duress to their parents. But obviously, the same thing is happening Arizona with respect to its new immigration law, which we will talk more about later.

Once again, as discussed earlier, the Ground Zero Mosque is another prime example of this mob mentality. Though not necessarily a state matter, it is certainly a local matter, and the attempt to dictate by majority opinion in this country what New York City and New York State ought to do is a good example of how we have gone off track. Obviously, people are entitled to their own opinions, but everyone from the media to other states to the federal government seem to feel they have a direct stake in the matter. And they feel that they are in a position to tell local governmental bodies in Lower Manhattan what should and shouldn't happen with property there. Some people have come to believe that because of what happened at Ground Zero, it has now become a national shrine, which gives everyone a stake in the discussion to influence and control everything that happens within blocks of the site. *But that is not the case.* We are all certainly entitled to our opinions, but what President Barack Obama, Newt Gingrich, the media, and the majority of Americans believe should not dictate the outcome. In accordance with our Constitution and the rule of law, the paramount role of governments, including the governing bodies in Lower Manhattan, is protection of life, liberty, and property, including property rights.

Unfortunately, because of precedents set during the Civil War, today virtually everything is subject to this type of majority mob rule. We have a federal government that is out of control and heedless of limitations or checks and balances as set forth in the Constitution. States have no respect for the sovereignty of other states. Governments have to our detriment lost sight of any semblance of independence or self-reliance. If a majority mob wants to tell New York City or Montana or Wyoming what they must do, members of that mob sincerely—but wrongfully—believe they have a right to do so.

Mob Rule Applied to Arizona Immigration Law

What is happening in Arizona regarding the enforcement of immigration laws is relevant to this discussion. Based on the prevailing mob-rule mentality, everyone seems to think they should be able to tell Arizona what to do. First of all, compelling arguments have been made that federal immigration policy is unconstitutional in the first place, and yet one more example of a federal attempt to assume powers well beyond those specifically granted in Article I, Section 8. Beyond all the huffing, puffing, and bluffing, however, the federal government's first reaction was, "Okay, then, it looks as though we're going to have to cut off federal funding and really hit you where it hurts." A number of other parties, who have no legitimate stake in the discussion, think they're also entitled to pile on and help whip Arizona into shape. We've got things so upside down and backward that we don't know which way is up.

We may not agree with Arizona. We may not like what they are doing there. We are entitled to have and express our opinions. We can all squawk all we want about it. But we've got to get away from thinking that the federal government, other states, the media, and other outsiders are entitled to push the individual states around and tell them what they can and can't and should and shouldn't do. Despite all the nonsense that has been knocked into our heads over the course of the past 150 years, the states are still entitled to some reasonable degree of self-determination. The states themselves are entitled to protection from mob rule and tyranny of the majority.

Inalienable rights are inalienable rights bestowed by our Creator in accordance with the laws of nature, and they are protected by the Constitution and the rule of law. If what Arizona has done violates individual liberties and the inalienable rights of people who are entitled to constitutional protection, then Arizona must be held accountable. But neither mob-rule democracy nor the heavy hand of the federal government provides proper checks or balances as outlined in our Constitution.

Inalienable rights are bestowed by our Creator and apply to everyone, but our Constitution protects the inalienable rights of U.S. citizens who have complied with the rule of law to attain that status and to be entitled to that protection. Exactly how the debate should end is beyond the scope of this discussion, but when the states, acting as a union, fail to take some kind of unified action on important issues such as immigration, why should the mob feel as though it's got the right to dictate what other states can and can't do? Instead, we the people and the states should be supporting Arizona in its exercise of the right of self-determination and state responsibility to do what it believes is in the best interests of the state.

While everyone may have an opinion, only those who live in Arizona, pay taxes there, vote there, and actually have to live with the consequences of whatever decisions the state makes have a real stake in the outcome. This is yet another example of the national mainstream media putting its spin on a local issue, stirring up controversy, and to a large degree completely misrepresenting what is actually going on.

Federal Supremacy

The federal government has supremacy only in those areas where the Constitution specifically gives it supremacy—not where it has unilaterally chosen to act. What the federal government and the president of the United States think should happen in Arizona or New York is irrelevant. *These are not federal issues!* Moreover, we need to quit thinking about a federal/state dichotomy. We need to start thinking in terms of we the people and of the states acting as individual states and as a union of states. Instead, the federal government has evolved into a completely disconnected entity with an agenda of its own that usually has nothing to do with what we the people and the states want, acting either individually or as a union. It is completely unaccountable to we the people and the states, as the parents and grandparents.

Relationships among the States

Though the federal government must be brought to heel, the states must likewise respect and take an arm's-length approach with sister states—particularly when there is no dispute among them. Most issues are not the same as the situation with the Colorado River and the Colorado River Compact, for example, which govern what happens with the water that flows from Colorado and Wyoming to the Pacific Ocean and how it is allocated among the states along its path. Just as with Wyoming and its wolves, what difference does it make what people in Massachusetts, for example, think about the compact? What happens to snowmelt from the Colorado Rockies is not their issue. Colorado is not their state. When Colorado is dealing with issues that have nothing to do with the states acting as a union, Massachusetts, New York and other states that have no dog in the fight should keep their noses out. Subject to the rule of law and inalienable, individual rights bestowed by the laws of nature and protected by the Constitution, a state should have the right to do what it deems best—subject to the terms and conditions of its own constitution. And if everyone else in the country wants to do something else, great! Let them do it! But let's stop drinking the poisoned Kool-Aid and thinking that everyone else is somehow entitled to tell Colorado, Wyoming, Arizona or Massachusetts what's best and acting as though the federal government is the big enforcer. That is a huge part of the problem that has gotten us to the precarious spot we're in. If this notion continues much further, nature will ultimately take its course, and eventually it won't to turn out the same way it did last time.

This is yet another example of how our progressive / federalist democracy has evolved into something completely beyond the scope of anything even our most ardent Federalist forebears ever envisioned or intended. They were talking about a glass or two of federal dominion wine with dinner. We're now drinking multiple bottles of federal-dominion port and democratic mob rule before breakfast! In the process, we've gotten ourselves into such a drunken stupor that we've lost all common sense, and we don't even realize it.

Municipal Land-Use Ordinances

Local government land-use ordinances have come to serve as yet another vehicle for government to infringe on inalienable private property rights via "the will of the majority." By this means, in many cases the urban majority seeks to impose its will on the rural minority, with little regard for private property rights.

Cities, towns, and communities across this country have been boiled like the proverbial frog, which was put in tepid water that was then gradually heated until the unwitting animal was finally cooked. Following the agenda and boilerplate paperwork handed to them, these local government entities have likewise gradually and many times unwittingly usurped inalienable, individual property rights—so slowly that both they and property owners have been unaware of what was happening. On that score, this next story is not unique.

39

Rosie McLayne and the New Zoning Ordinance

As a busy mother and a work-from-home paralegal for a large law firm, Rosie McLayne has a full schedule. Two days a week she commutes nearly over fifty miles from her rural home to her office in a large city; on the other days, she telecommutes and is perhaps even busier. An avid gardener and runner, the striking and amiable Rosie is also active in community theater. Although she never had much interest in politics, she is now a mainstay in community events. Despite the demands of her hectic schedule, when Rosie heard the local town council was considering adoption of a new zoning and land-use ordinance, she decided to attend the introductory meeting. After she attended a nearly vacant town meeting where the changes were proposed, she decided she wanted to know more. After carefully reading the proposed ordinance, Rosie was incensed.

The first thing she noticed was that not even a well-educated and experienced paralegal was capable of readily understanding the document. But the worst thing was that the ordinance stated that the ordinance itself was now the source of all property rights and that property owners could do nothing with their property except those things specifically listed as "permitted uses." The ordinance sought to restrict almost all forms of production. It also sought to limit animal rights and to prohibit home business. In addition, it sought to elevate form over substance, prioritize appearances, create a special place for everything, and install a new board that could veto any construction that was not aesthetically pleasing or that was "out of character" with the surrounding neighborhood. In terms of heavy-handedness, it also made any violations of the ordinance criminal offenses with stiff sentences, including fines and jail time.

Rosie quickly alerted her neighbors, most of whom had heard nothing of the ordinance before she brought it to their attention.

After much debate and discussion, a small group of neighbors persuaded the town council to instruct the zoning board to postpone any recommendation for six months to allow town residents sufficient time to study and understand the proposed ordinance. Rosie, along with other proactive residents, then organized education workshops to thoroughly review the proposed ordinance and provide informed comments to the zoning board and town council. Their efforts resulted in over fifty written comments that objected on a number of grounds to the proposed ordinance.

As they debated the ordinance with the mayor and the zoning board chairman, the concerned neighbors argued that the ordinance violated the inherent and inalienable property rights of property owners. "But what about the town's rights? What about the inherent, inalienable rights of the community?" the zoning board chairman wanted to know. Rosie stood to respond. "Contrary to what you must think, government does not have inherent, inalienable rights," she said. "Such rights are based on the laws of nature and nature's God. They are gifts from God that existed before governments existed, before laws existed, before the Constitution existed, while governments and their laws are man-made entities. Any power and authority that governments have come from the people—and that is exactly the point: we have not given this government the authority to infringe upon our inherent, inalienable property rights."

At that point Nick Romero, Rosie's friend and insistent neighbor, took the floor and added, "The primary role and function of government is to protect and defend people's inherent and inalienable God-given rights of life, liberty, and property!"

"Regardless," said the mayor, "this ordinance is what is best for the town. We know what is best, and it is our responsibility to make the law. As your elected representatives, it's our decision to make. Besides, most of the people in this town don't have any problem with this ordinance."

This discussion started a long process that ultimately involved many discussions and heated exchanges over the course of the next three years. Based on general opposition to the ordinance, the council chamber was often packed when it was discussed. Based on the intense opposition to the ordinance, including from Rosie, Nick and their neighbors, the town council ultimately tried to out-wait the opposition. Finally, at the end of a quiet meeting when almost no one was in attendance, an one of the council members absent, a majority of the council passed the ordinance under the "unfinished business" item on the agenda. Further incensed by the council's tactics, Rosie, and her group were not ready to give up. Rosie quickly researched and prepared the necessary paperwork to file a referendum petition based on applicable state law, to refer the new ordinance to a vote of the people. The small group of community members worked together to increase their numbers and gather the signatures of about 60 percent of the registered voters in the community (doubling the 30 percent legally required), requesting that the new ordinance be put to a vote of the people via a referendum election.

At this point, Rosie's story and the issues she was confronting started converging with other situations in other communities around the state, including another community along the front range about 90 miles away. In that community, a wealthy doctor owned a large piece of hillside property that he intended to develop. The doctor had a clear understanding of how politics works; he didn't live in the community and didn't care what his neighbors thought, but he was on great terms with many members of the state assembly to whom he pledged generous campaign contributions. As part of his medical practice, he offered free screenings and other services to legislators, and he had developed a cozy relationship with many state lawmakers. When the residents of the town took the position that his development plans violated the existing land-use ordinance, he used all his connections to flex his political muscle through state legislators to coerce the local council to change its ordinance. This sparked outrage among neighbors and town residents, who quickly gathered more than enough signatures to challenge the change by referendum. Before the referendum could go to a vote, though, the doctor's friends in the state assembly intervened to pass a new state law prohibiting any change to local land-use ordinances by initiative or referendum anywhere in the state.

With that new law in place (but on appeal to the state's supreme court), Rosie and her neighbors filed their own referendum petition. Although both the land-use ordinance and the new state law should obviously be found unconstitutional and struck down, we have had enough experience in the system to know better than to take anything for granted. But we'll check in on Rosie and her neighbors again later.

The Political, Elitist Agenda

In addition to the evolution of democratic mob rule and the intrusive fourth branch of government, heavy-handed aristocracy has returned to America to control the governing class and impose economic insanity. One recent example of this is the passage of healthcare reform legislation by members of Congress, who exempted themselves and their families. While the legislation was pitched as being a benefit primarily to the middle class and those who can't afford health insurance, obviously there is a conglomerate of special interests who will benefit most financially from it—with little quid pro quo paid for that benefit. While this is just one example of what happens, the big picture reality is that our socio-economic structure has now evolved to the point that a very wealthy class of less than 10 percent of the people in this country own more than 90 percent of the wealth. And who do you think essentially control our elected leaders and politicians? Now consider the fact that many of our elected leaders are professional, career politicians, who develop very cozy relationships with the wealthy elite who fund their perpetual campaigns. Many politicians now represent a second or third generation in office or have been in office for multiple terms—some for as long as thirty years or more.

Now, couple all this with the fact that the two major political parties, acting in collusion with the ruling class (made up of big business interests and an elite group of wealthy Americans), set the agenda and give political marching orders to our elected leaders. And they are not very benevolent rulers. We have learned from experience on both sides of the aisle that it is easy to spend money that does not belong to you, especially when you never need to worry about paying it back personally. Money and power corrupt and, sadly, there is much corruption in our system. King George would be proud. It has been said, "If General Charles Cornwallis and King George III were fighting to keep control of the American colonies today, six of the last seven presidents would have been right in the middle of the fight—on their side, trying to keep power centralized for the elite."

Fruits of the Agenda

The primary agenda of this ruling elite that controls both parties is to further consolidate power and limit freedom of choice (otherwise known as liberty) in a wide variety of fundamental ways. In the process, these people seek to eliminate personal responsibility, remove risk through unending regulation, shield people from the natural consequences of their actions, all while seeking to avoid all accountability for their own actions. One state governor recently lamented that one of his biggest problems is fighting the federal government in its efforts to absolve everyone of their personal responsibilities.

This agenda has resulted in a long list of government *entitlements*, resulting in a wide variety of unfunded liabilities and a series of government Ponzi schemes worse than anything Bernie Madoff ever dreamed up, including Social Security, Medicare, the prescription drug programs, No Child Left Behind, and a long list of government welfare programs. Although the federal government wants to manage essentially everything, its own woeful track record of mismanagement speaks for itself.

The Two-Party "Situation"

One major political hurdle for Americans today is the fact that a majority of us simply have no effective voice or representation in government. We can call our government a democracy, representative democracy, constitutional republic, or whatever we want, but that doesn't change reality. Political policy in this country—particularly at the national level but also at the state and local levels—is no longer directed by we the people, the electorate. Our elected leaders no longer listen to us or pay much, if any, attention to what we say—even if we claim major party affiliation and ideology. Our governments are no longer accountable to the people. *In American politics today policy is almost completely dictated by the two major political parties and their internal agendas.* These agendas are not directed by the people or even by a majority of party members but by power-party elites, big business, and bureaucrats.

When did we go from being a government "of the people, by the people, for the people" to a government "of the party, by the party, for the party"?

A growing number of Americans now identify themselves as Independents who do not identify or affiliate with either of the two major political parties, which means that party politicians do not even pretend to represent them and their views. Regardless of any purported differences in their agendas, the two major political parties have an absolute stranglehold on American politics and policy. Together they act as the single biggest obstacle to any meaningful foundational reform or change in this country.

Whatever the two major political parties may have stood for historically is essentially irrelevant today. What do they stand for now? Does either of the parties really stand for limited government, increased liberty, or even a dedication to upholding the Constitution? Does either of the parties really stand for protection of fundamental inalienable, individual rights? According to one observer, "The Democrats are the party that says government will make you smarter, taller, richer, and remove the crabgrass in your lawn. The Republicans are the party that says government doesn't work and then they get elected and prove it!" Another says, "The only difference between the Democrats and the Republicans is that the Democrats allow the poor to be corrupt too." As our friend Worth says, "Arguing about Republicans versus Democrats is the same as arguing about Coke versus Pepsi. Sure, they have their subtle taste differences, but at the end of the day, they are both just sugar-poison colas!"

Similar to ill-mannered teenagers, both sides of our current two-party system spend the vast majority of their time bickering, squawking, criticizing, and pointing fingers at the other side. They spend more time and effort fighting than trying to accomplish anything productive. More loyal to party association than anything else, including principle, even the best elected leaders seem to be so hamstrung by partisan politics that they are largely ineffective. Those who aren't completely brainwashed are kicked to the curb, isolated, and marginalized, leaving few who are willing to buck their party to be a legitimate voice of reason.

The vast majority of our elected leaders seem to be more concerned about helping satiate their party's thirst for power than they are about anything else. As a well-known world statesman once said, "Few men change their party for the sake of their principles; many change their principles for the sake of their party." We saw this in the last presidential election. With few exceptions, even those who had previously developed their own, individual brand quickly fell in line and kowtowed to the party platform in order to have a shot at getting elected—or even just nominated for the election.

APPROPRIATE FEDERAL GOV'T

THE TWO PARTIES   THE MEDIA   NEW 4TH BRANCH OF GOV'T

TODAY'S FEDERAL GOVERNMENT

Even if we could determine the true, core ideology of the two existing power parties—a virtual impossibility—it all gets lost in the squall. The old saying about lawyers is true: "A town that can't support one lawyer can always support two." Why? Because with two lawyers around to bicker and fight, they can always stir things up enough that they will both have plenty of business. As a general rule, the same is true of the two major political power parties in this country. They take a stand against the politics of the other mostly to justify their own existence. Any actual ideology gets lost in all the smoke and dust they create, and most of the show is largely just a circus act to distract and entertain the American people while the ship of state cruises deftly through the fog. Who's to say most of it is not just a big show? Those who have seen it close up know that for the most part it is.

The Tail Is Wagging the Dog

In a country as big and diverse as the United States, it is absurd to think that two major political parties represent the views of 90 percent of all Americans. In fact, according to recent polls, as many as 60 percent of Americans identify themselves as Independents. What this means is that if 60 percent are Independents, only 40 percent actually identify with the two major parties. In other words, probably no more than 25 percent of the American people actually relate to either one of the major governing parties. But those parties, together, control this country politically. They are the epitome of the tail wagging the dog. For many people, choosing between the two major parties is the same as choosing between a rattlesnake and a cobra. As many as 60 percent of the people vote for the "lesser of two evils" and have virtually no effective voice in the current political system.

Hindsight Is 20/20

Hindsight has proven 20/20 with respect to our major political parties and the concerns of our Founding Fathers. Political parties did not exist in 1789. Although there were various factions of political thought at the time the Constitution was written, organized parties had not yet taken the political stage. Even the original Federalist/Anti-Federalist debate was not driven by political parties, and many of the Founding Fathers were very concerned about the formation of such. One of the most revered of the Founding Fathers, George Washington, said this in his farewell address:

"[Political parties] serve to organize faction, to give it an artificial and extraordinary force; to put, in the place of the delegated will of the nation, the will of a party, often a small but artful and enterprising minority of the community; and, according to the alternate triumphs of different parties, to make the public administration the mirror of the ill-concerted and incongruous projects of faction, rather than the organ of consistent and wholesome plans digested by common counsels, and modified by mutual interests.

"However [political parties] may now and then answer popular ends, they are likely, in the course of time and things, to become potent engines, by which cunning, ambitious, and unprincipled men will be enabled to subvert the power of the people, and to usurp for themselves the reins of government; destroying afterwards the very engines, which have lifted them to unjust dominion."

We the People Have Been Displaced

The two major parties occupy the political position that we the people and the states—the effectual parents and grandparents, the intended leaders of our governments—were originally intended to occupy. Today our beloved grandchild has grown to be a belligerent and disrespectful man-child because we have let him. He has kicked us to the curb and has replaced us with a whole new family: the major political parties—a gang of thugs equivalent to the mafia. The unruly grandchild is no longer accountable to his parents and, ultimately, his grandparents—we the people. Instead of respecting us, he abuses us, takes over the house, and runs up the credit cards, all while coercing us into cleaning up his mess. And when a rival gang or the bill collector comes to kick in the door, guess who's going to get caught in the crossfire? We are!

The Bottom Line Regarding the Two Major Parties

In short, the two major power parties have failed this country. They have failed the American people. They have put us and kept us on an indisputable collision course with the laws of nature, and we're quickly approaching the rocks that will sink our ship. Nevertheless, both power parties shy away from any real change or improvement, instead putting more Band-Aids on symptoms, applying more cosmetics to the equation, and pushing our problems forward for another generation to solve. The bottom line is that these two parties have been responsible for getting us into the spot we're in, and there is no credible reason to believe they will get us out.

It is time for us—we the people—to stand up and shout, "Enough!" We need to find and support real leaders who are willing to stand up to the parties. We need to insist upon principled elected officials who stand above the fray with integrity and who espouse solid principles above power politics and party conformity. In today's political landscape, such individuals are rare exceptions to the rule. Regrettably, they do not represent the general political populace. So while our goal is to champion such leaders, it is not to defend or muster further support for either of the two major political parties.

Given the profound lack of allegiance to the people they are meant to serve, it is time for a vote of no confidence for both parties in the current two-party system as well as a veto of the pack mentality that controls our corrupt political system. It is time we the people take back this country and restore a government of the people, by the people, for the people.

We the People Have Let This Happen

The recitation of tales of unjust, governmental dominion could go on and on, but the bottom line is we the people have let this happen! For decades we have failed to hold our governments and elected leaders accountable. It is not government alone that has gone astray. With the government's help and encouragement, we as individuals have also lost much of our moral compass. We have lost our vision and work ethic. We consume more than we produce, we refuse to live within our means, and we have become dependent. Our sense of community is eroding. A gluttonous entertainment culture has become prevalent. We have become apathetic and distracted. We go along just to get along and assume that someone else will take care of the problem.

Thomas Jefferson, one of our best-known and most respected Founding Fathers said, "If a nation expects to be ignorant and free . . . it expects what never was and never will be."

Much of what is going on today began many decades and many generations ago. Just as in constructing a building, it began as a plan. Some lawmakers, presidents, and bankers have spent years dreaming these scenarios into being. They have employed architects to put their thoughts on paper in the form of legislation and government programs. Their planning has been extensive—and they're still working on it. Now their nefarious schemes are becoming reality.

In this discussion, we have focused mostly on the federal government, yet the states are just as guilty of building the administrative fourth branch. Nevertheless, if there is a legitimate place for the fourth branch of government, it is in the states—created by the states, funded by the states, and run by the states. But it was surely never meant to be the massive, overwhelming federal monstrosity it has become.

By now we should be able to clearly see that Progressivism is the agenda behind all this. Arguably, the seeds of Progressivism were planted by the original Federalists. Over the years those seeds germinated, put down roots, and have grown, bloomed, blossomed, and now morphed and mutated into a federal government monster that bears little resemblance to anything even the most ardent Federalists envisioned. At this point, Progressivism has now been well cultivated by both parties. At this point, we do disservice to the term and concept of federalism by even associating it with what has happened. Today, Progressivism much more accurately describes what has happened—and is still happening—more aggressively than ever.

Chapter 5

A Few Examples of Governmental Heavy-handedness and Abuse

We have just described some of the political and governmental structural developments that have occurred over the course of the past 220 years. Now we're going to tell some true stories that describe the net effects of these developments.

Government Has become Abusive and Heavy-handed at All Levels

In conjunction with out-of-control administrative growth, those same government entities have become heavy-handed. The blame for this lies largely with we the people. Instead of keeping a careful watch over growing government tentacles, we chose to look the other way, or worse, we opted for intrusion over responsibility despite the dangers. We chose to pick up the snake. Government, as George Washington warned, is like fire. He called it "a dangerous servant and a fearful master."

We knew the inherent nature of government even as we acquiesced, but all the programs, all the complacency, all the safety seemed okay. We have come to embrace it; we have trusted it and allowed it to gain advantage over us. Now we hang on because we don't know how to let go, keeping it close where it can do a lot of damage despite a vague or even sure knowledge that there is menace behind the mask.

Certainly we are not the first people to be fooled by a government snake. In Germany before World War II, many people sensed that something was wrong, even in the calm security and routine of everyday life. But in the smallest increments, a vice was being tightened on their lives. What at first seemed like minor inconveniences quickly grew into powerful governmental bonds. Whisperings of governmental abuses were ignored until they became governmental horrors. Many citizens remained complacent about control until it was simply too late. By the time they could not longer ignore it, it was too big to stop.

What follows are stories of the growing heavy-handedness and resulting conflict between we the people and federal, state, and local governments. Though there are many well-known stories of governmental abuses, we're going to highlight a smattering of stories that may not be quite as well known. As you read these accounts, ask: What abuses are we ignoring? And how do the principles of the laws of nature and common sense apply?

The United States of America v. Maggie Rawlins

The first story involves a woman named Maggie Rawlins. Before Maggie's husband's untimely death, they were running a ranching operation in eastern Arizona on some of the most rugged, remote, and inhospitable country in the lower forty-eight states. The ranch they operated was located entirely on "public land"—land owned by we the people of the United States and managed by the Department of the Interior through the Bureau of Land Management (BLM). Owned by the federal government and divided into grazing "allotments," this was land left over from the homesteading era that no one had claimed. Maggie and her husband put the land, forage, and water to beneficial use, utilizing it to raise livestock under a "grazing permit." Although the land is "owned" by we the people and "managed" by the federal government, if not for the Rawlinses and their ranching operation, the land would be essentially barren and unproductive, put to no beneficial use.

After her husband was killed in a horse wreck on the ranch, it was all Maggie could do to operate and maintain the ranch by herself, with a little part-time help from family, friends and neighbors. When a national monument was created that encompassed the entire ranch, life really changed for Maggie—and not for the better. Land that had long been ignored by the BLM now became a focal point, and Maggie was subjected to continual harassment by the BLM. Eventually, it became obvious that the BLM was determined to put her out of business and move her off the land. Although it was suitable for cattle grazing, by any other objective standard the ranch and surrounding area were essentially godforsaken desert. But under the pretext of drought conditions, the BLM sent Maggie a letter stating that all her cattle had to be removed from the ranch by a certain date or be subject to confiscation by the BLM.

Maggie had no place to go. Because of the remoteness, lack of access, and rugged terrain, it would be difficult, if not impossible, to gather her cattle from the main high plateau where they grazed in the summertime. Had it been late fall, the cattle would start to come down on their own and could be gathered, but the BLM would not wait until fall. They demanded that all cattle be removed by the end of August. Maggie was in a serious bind, so she called Ross "Mac" MacMasterson, a retired attorney and former partner of our friend Mancos MacLeod, who had helped Maggie and her husband years earlier.

MacMasterson first attempted to reason with the BLM. He elicited the assistance of a well-respected older generation BLM manager who had always demonstrated a lot of common sense and understanding. This manager attempted to work within the agency to mediate a satisfactory resolution, but to no avail. Agency bosses said they were under orders from the top, and were unyielding in their agenda and marching orders. They wanted Maggie's cattle off the range immediately. But the manager did manage to secure commitments for a wide range of expensive BLM assistance *if Maggie would remove her cattle.* This agency manager, who at the end of the day was supposed to be a servant to the people, was so disgusted by what the BLM was doing, its tactics, and how it was handling the whole situation that he took early retirement and left the BLM.

Mac then contemplated initiating litigation to seek an injunction, but like his former partner, Mancos MacLeod, he had become jaded and had little faith in the so-called justice system. Mac knew that the legal system was ill-equipped to handle Maggie's unique situation. He knew from vast experience that the thing the justice system was most effective at was consuming resources—resources that Maggie Rawlins didn't have. Mac knew it could consume tens, even hundreds of thousands of dollars, and take years before anything was sorted out. Meanwhile, Maggie had no money, and the only way she could get money to live or pay attorneys was from the sale of the cattle she was fighting to save.

"If you'd broken a law, I could get you off — but you violated a *Federal guideline!*"

With few other viable options, and with the BLM dangling all kinds of carrots to unduly influence her decision, Maggie decided to attempt to gather her cattle. A crew of sympathetic cowboys and ranchers came to Maggie's aid. Even Mac MacMasterson saddled up and went along. After several weeks of hard riding, barely half of the cattle had been gathered off the rugged plateau. At that point, the BLM, without a court order or any due process of law, ordered Maggie and her cowboys off the ranch.

While Mac explored further legal and administrative options, the BLM sought to gather, impound and remove all remaining cattle. At first the BLM tried to gather the cattle using somewhat traditional means. A crew of BLM bureaucrats and mercenary cowboys attempted to gather the rest of the cattle in a massive operation that ended in dismal failure. The government then spent hundreds of thousands of dollars trying to *helicopter net* the cattle, which resulted in only mixed success. When they finally got part of the herd into a corral, the BLM transported the cattle without any regard for state livestock identification and transporation laws. It was their position that because of the Supremacy Clause, as a branch of the federal government, they were exempt from any applicable state laws, including livestock brand, identification, and transportation laws. While Maggie's case languished in the administrative process and legal system, the BLM took the cattle to the nearest livestock auction to be sold.

Maggie, Mac MacMasterson, and a supporting cast of neighboring ranchers showed up at the auction to try to buy the cattle back. They had made signs to inform other ranchers and cattle buyers at the sale what was actually going on. At that point, the BLM canceled the sale and informed the local county sheriff that he was responsible for securing, feeding, and caring for the cattle until the BLM could decide what to do. Maggie felt helpless. Mac put in a call to the county attorney. They discussed the U.S. Supreme Court case *Printz & Mack v. The United States.* The *Printz* case is a truly landmark but little known Tenth Amendment case (that we'll talk more about later) in which the court held that the federal government has no constitutional authority to impart orders to a county sheriff.

By the time Mac got back to the auction, the sheriff had talked to the county attorney and told Mac that he wasn't accepting orders from the BLM anymore—and that he wasn't taking responsibility for the cattle. "What you do with the cattle is up to you," the sheriff told Mac, "but we're not going to be put in the middle of it."

On Mac's advice, Maggie secured a brand inspection on the impounded cattle in accordance with applicable state laws. With the cattle thus identified as hers, Maggie and the other ranchers loaded them up to take home. They were ecstatic! Things had turned out much better than they could have ever expected.

Early the next morning, their enthusiasm came to an abrupt end when Maggie, Mac, and the ranchers' wives started receiving messages from the U.S. Attorney's Office threatening federal prison terms and $250,000 fines for "stealing federal property." The messages detailed a

number of other related charges, including aiding, abetting, and conspiracy. The wives, with tears streaming down their faces and panic in
their voices, passed the news along to their husbands. It was hard to
know what to do. The Feds were driving a hard bargain, and although
Mac didn't believe they had a legal leg to stand on, that didn't stop them
from making serious threats to coerce the ranchers to roll over and give
the cattle back.

When the ranchers didn't immediately cave in, the FBI was at their
doorstep with well-practiced intimidation tactics. Still, Mac MacMasterson, Maggie, and the ranchers stood their ground. As nervous as they
were, the ranchers relied on Mac's judgment and followed his lead, cre-
ating a standoff for weeks. The U.S. Attorney's Office launched a full
media blitz against the ranchers, casting them as vigilante outlaws who
had "taken the law into their own hands" and characterizing the sheriff
as a rogue with no respect for the rule of law.

Despite the precedent articulated in the *Printz* case, most of the
elected officials in Maggie's own county did little to support her and the
local ranchers. State and local government leaders were largely intimidated by the federal government, and their timid response was, "We'd
love to help, but we have to work with these people. We've got to go
along to get along, and we simply can't survive around here without
federal grants and financial support."

Maggie and her small band of ranchers felt like David going against
Goliath. It was difficult for the ranchers and their families to weigh the
risks and stand their ground. Under threats and ultimatums, fearing the
Feds were laying groundwork to justify a more forceful—perhaps even
violent—pounce, they waited.

Like a high-noon showdown in an old western movie, the sheriff (local officials) and the townspeople had effectively cleared the
street, afraid of the federal bully with the big guns. In this modern-day
example, many local leaders were so intimidated by the federal government on one hand and so co-opted on the other hand that they didn't
dare raise their voices in support. Among other things, they feared losing federal grants and program funding they had become dependent
upon. In an area dominated by federal *public* land—land, in fact, that

is owned by we the people—local leaders had become so accustomed to going along just to get along that they did not dare say or do anything that might cause them to get crossways with the federal government.

In the end, the government did not employ tactics used in places such as Waco, Texas, and Ruby Ridge, Idaho, but the wait was intense because how were Maggie and the ranchers to know how far the government would go? The ranchers and their families could have easily woken up to an army of drawn guns in their faces after their doors had been kicked in at dawn by federal agents.

Sound far-fetched? If you think so, talk to residents of rural San Juan County, New Mexico, who were accused of violating federal antiquities laws on public lands.

An Amassed Army of Federal Agents

In the spring of 2009, following a sting operation, in total disregard for local law enforcement and applicable state laws, federal authorities amassed an army of hundreds of federal agents and dozens of vehicles in a predawn raid, kicking in doors with no-knock warrants and arresting citizens in their beds at gunpoint for nonviolent crimes—citizens who under the U.S. Constitution are presumed innocent until proven guilty.

This was not a drug raid. It had no ties to the War on Terror. There were no violent criminals involved or serious flight risks. Yet, surrounded by swarms of federal agent storm troopers, these people were physically dragged from their homes and hauled away in handcuffs while their children looked on in shock and horror. Over twenty people in the community and surrounding areas were arrested in this manner. As soon as they were able to post bail and be released from custody, two of those arrested (including a prominent and much-loved local doctor) committed suicide rather than continue to be dogged, humiliated and treated this way by the federal government. In the end, not a single one of those arrested that morning received a prison sentence, and the government's own star witness also committed suicide.

In both this case and the Maggie Rawlins' case, it was not the DEA, ICE, INS, IRS, ATF, FBI, CIA or other federal agency normally associated with such brutal tactics that was responsible for these actions. It was the Department of the Interior, the unconstitutional fourth branch administrative department responsible for oversight of the Bureau of Indian Affairs (and mismanagement of the Native American Trust Fund), Bureau of Reclamation, and Bureau of Land Mismanagement. It was in its capacity as a land and resource management agency (BLM)—for *we the people*—that it engaged in such thuggish and heavy-handed tactics typically thought possible only in totalitarian regimes like the Third Reich or Stalin's Soviet Union. In both cases, this happened with little, if any, accountability for agency actions.

Obviously, when an administrative land management agency feels comfortable going this far over the top; when our government's heavy-handed tactics start putting good but imperfect people completely over the edge; the federal government is completely out of control.

Questions we need to be continually asking are: "Where are the checks and balances?" and "Where is the accountability?"

Meanwhile, Back at Maggie's Ranch

To conclude the Maggie Rawlins story, the federal government ended up spending hundreds of thousands of taxpayer dollars trying to round up the cattle left on Maggie's ranch—cattle that would have left the high country on their own in a matter of weeks. After warning Maggie not to set foot on the ranch again, and after threatening Maggie, her attorney, and the ranchers with long prison terms and enormous fines for "stealing government property," the BLM secretly sent government contractors to the ranch in helicopters to shoot any remaining cattle, leaving them dead for the coyotes and crows to clean up.

Having successfully driven her off the land, without any meaningful accountability whatsoever, the BLM then made it virtually impossible for Maggie to sell, or anyone else to successfully operate, what was left of her ranching operation. In the end, Maggie Rawlins, a once tough-as-nails, free-spirited, freedom-loving American—a one-of-a-kind maverick to be sure—died as a broken and destitute woman at the ripe old age of 55.

Another Special Case

In any discussion of heavy-handed federal government abuses, the discussion wouldn't be complete without some mention of perhaps the biggest oppressor of all from the administrative branch: the Internal Revenue Service.

Before we take the gloves off, let's begin with a premise that we should all be able to agree upon: we the people have a contractual obligation through the Constitution to support the core functions of government. In return, the government has a contractual obligation to protect, defend, and preserve our fundamental individual rights, including life, liberty, and property.

Now the big question: Who's doing the better job of upholding its side of the bargain?

A second and obvious premise that we should also all be able to agree upon is that the Internal Revenue Code is ridiculously and needlessly complicated! Aside from being demonstrably abusive in their collection and enforcement tactics, IRS codes and policies mutilate the intent of the constitutional directive to support the government we created.

For this part of the discussion, we're going to borrow a tale from another writer that we think sums up the situation well:

In 1998, after several IRS employees blew the whistle, Congress decided to put on another dog-and-pony show to quench the political heat they were taking as a result of numerous articles and public outcries regarding IRS crimes and abuses. During the hearings, Jennifer Long, along with several other IRS employees, testified under oath that the IRS routinely fabricated evidence against American citizens who the IRS knew were financially incapable of defending themselves against the relentless and ruthless IRS.

One IRS agent testified, "If the American people knew all that was going on inside the IRS, there would be a revolt tomorrow." Another IRS employee was so afraid of retaliation from his employer and our government that he testified silhouetted behind a lighted screen with his voice muffled to conceal his identity. Protecting a witness in such a manner in front of Congress had happened only once before, when a former member of the Mafia exposed his fellow thugs. (Any similarities between the

IRS and the Mafia are purely intentional!). It was revealed that many victims of IRS fraud had been ruined for life: some went to prison, others lost everything, others sought refuge by moving abroad, and others committed suicide. Yet the U.S. Congress did nothing to protect its own people from such abuse and future IRS crimes. Congress's reaction, after hearing all these violations of the law and the public trust, was to order IRS employees to become more "user friendly" and to open their offices on Saturdays.

In the spirit of acknowledging minor, superficial improvements, if you call or visit an IRS service center today, there is a good chance you will be impressed with the friendliness and helpfulness of its customer service representatives. To put on a more *user-friendly* front, the IRS has indeed improved its customer service. In fact, IRS customer service representatives may seem so friendly and helpful that you will feel completely comfortable when they attempt to solicit your bank account and asset information.

Some time later, the writer of the foregoing tale was in Washington, D.C., to receive a national award. At one meeting, this gentleman leaned over to the Senate majority leader and asked, "When are you guys going to do something about the Gestapo in America?" Without hesitation, the senator replied, "You're referring to the IRS? That will never happen; even *we* kowtow to the IRS." He paused and added, "Remember, that's who pays our salaries and for everything else in the government." The writer reminded the majority leader that it is actually the people who pay Senate salaries and everything else in the government and that the IRS is one of the many administrative components of the government, which was never meant to be.

Just as the Federal Reserve has done, the IRS has fooled the entire U.S. citizenry. The Founders—including the Federalists—never intended that there would be a tax on income. The Sixteenth Amendment, which supposedly authorized Congress to impose such a tax, was arguably never properly ratified by the states. Nonetheless, the tax is fiercely upheld, and IRS collection and enforcement methods are astonishingly ruthless. According to credible sources, this single entity confiscates more homes, destroys more families, takes more money, and ruins more lives in America than all the terrorists, mafia, drug dealers, and street gangs combined.

Even as we are writing, the following news story caught our attention:

"The Internal Revenue Service (IRS) intends to purchase sixty Remington Model 870 Police RAMAC #24587 12-gauge pump-action shotguns for the Criminal Investigation Division. The Remington parkerized shotguns, with fourteen-inch barrel, modified choke, Wilson Combat Ghost Ring rear sight and XS4 contour bead front sight, Knoxx Reduced Recoil adjustable stock, and speed-feed ribbed black forend, are designated as the only shotguns authorized for IRS duty based on compatibility with IRS existing shotgun inventory, certified armor and combat training and protocol, maintenance, and parts."

It should be startlingly obvious that we can no longer depend on the federal government to provide protection and security for its own people. As the IRS continues to commit crimes against innocent citizens, it is living proof that the greatest threat we face as a nation is our own federal government.

They're Just Getting Started

The federal government recently announced plans to build a new National Security Agency spy center in Utah. This massive, multibillion dollar spy center is said to have roof space as big as some small towns. It will consume enough electricity to power a city of a million people. It is hard to imagine all the private sector companies that will be co-opted in this venture. Collusion between the NSA and cell phone companies for domestic spying is old news (partnerships between the NSA and several large IT companies is likewise well known), but who else is in on the spy game? The NSA is developing several such spy centers throughout the United States. These ventures raise a number of questions: What is the role of Congress in all this? Who has oversight? What is its purpose? Where is the accountability? Does this instill greater confidence in the federal government? Do we feel safer? Will we *be* safer?

In Utah's case, most state and local political leaders seem to be ecstatic about the opportunities for economic stimulus and job growth, much as Nevada must have been about the establishment and growth of the Nevada Test Site back in the 1950s, '60s, and '70s. At the time, Nevada had little concern over nuclear fallout; that would come later. This was yet another naive yielding to the federal government's continual refrain of "Just trust us."

As we consider where to place our trust, consider Executive Order 13528, signed by President Obama on January 11, 2010. This order establishes a council of ten regional governors who will coordinate and control all federal government and military control over the United States, answering to the secretary of defense, who in turn answers to the president. Do these ten governors correlate with the ten Federal Emergency Management Agency regions? To whom are they ultimately accountable, and where does accountability to the people factor in? Where is our representation in the decisions made by this council? Your guess is as good as ours.

Other Examples of Heavy-handedness

Despite banking disasters on Wall Street and the establishment of spy centers in the West, we are not grand conspiracy theorists, but our trust in our government has more than waned. Outrageous abuses such as those that occurred at Waco, Texas, and in Ruby Ridge, Idaho, are not things of the past, nor do they occur just at the federal level.

In the spring of 2008, acting on a false anonymous tip, Texas State Police stormed a tight-knit religious community in West Texas and ripped four hundred children, including nursing infants, from their parents and their homes. A nationwide media frenzy ensued. Spin doctors painted the community as composed of religious zealots, uncaring of women and children. But as with the dark portrayal of the "vigilantes" who "stole" Maggie's cattle back, the tale was mostly spin. At first justified by a Texas trial court, the abusive actions of Texas Child Protective Services were quickly struck down by Texas appellate courts. After months of separation and heartache, the children were finally returned to their families, their safe haven restored. But the children and their families were left traumatized.

According to a recent article in *Readers Digest,* this is just the tip of the iceberg. The use of SWAT teams and storm troopers has been on the rise for some time, but in the past ten years, there has been an explosion in the use of these tactics against American citizens entitled to a constitutional presumption of innocence. Government strong-arm tactics now penetrate every corner of the country.

According to the article, "Local police departments once reserved SWAT teams for crises like hostage standoffs. Now they're involving them in community policing, using them for intimidation, and sending them on house searches to arrest people for nonviolent crimes." With all the misidentification and mistakes that occur, innocent people endure nightmares of this nature on a regular basis.

In just one of a handful of recent examples, SWAT teams misread an address, kicked in a door, and rousted a seventy-something couple out of bed, forcing the husband to the floor at gunpoint. In another case, they mistakenly bashed in the door of an innocent thirty-three-year-old man, handcuffed him, and interrogated him at gunpoint for fifteen minutes before discovering their mistake—and then they refused to pay for a new door. In another case, they raided a wrong house and impounded the vehicle of a family that was fitted with special equipment and a special car seat for a disabled three-year-old boy.

Drug War, War on Terror . . . Food War . . . What Next?

Then there's this story, which was essentially ignored by the mainstream media. According to independent reports, in December 2008, a state SWAT team, armed with semiautomatic rifles and acting in conjunction with state agencies under the direction of federal agents, invaded the home of a family in Pennsylvania. They herded the family onto the couches in the living room and kept guns trained on parents, children, toddlers, and infants from approximately 11 a.m. to 8 p.m. According to firsthand witnesses, members of the team were aggressive and belligerent, and the children were traumatized. At some point, the first SWAT team was relieved by another team that tried to befriend the family.

This family had run a large, well-known food cooperative storehouse for many years on the western side of the same city where our Constitution was born. During the raid, agents from the Department of Agriculture were present. The search warrant was reported to be suspicious looking, but agents began rifling through all of the family's possessions, a task that lasted hours and resulted in a complete upheaval of every private area in the home. Many items were taken that were not listed on the search warrant. The family was not permitted a phone call, and they were not advised as to what crime they were being accused of. They were not read their rights. Agents took ten thousand dollars worth of food, including the family's personal stock of food for the coming year. All of their computers and all of their cell phones were also taken, as well as phone and contact records. The food cooperative was virtually shut down. There was no rational explanation or justification for this extreme violation of constitutional rights. Presumably the proprietors of this food co-op storehouse might eventually be charged with running a retail establishment without a license. Why then the Gestapo-type invasion and interrogation for a third-degree misdemeanor charge?

According to some, this incident has raised the ominous specter of a restrictive new era in regulation and enforcement regarding the nation's private food supply. This same type of abusive search and seizure was reported by innocents who fell victim to oppressive federal drug laws passed in the 1990s. The present circumstance raises some obvious questions: Is there some rabid new interpretation of an existing drug law that considers food a controlled substance worthy of a nasty SWAT team operation? Or worse, is there a previously unrecognized provision pertaining to food in Homeland Security regulations? Some have attributed this operation to an out-of-control, rogue, Rambo-type agent; if so, this would be a best-case scenario. Any other explanation might spell the beginning of the end of the freedom to eat unregulated and unmonitored (government-approved) food.

According to sources close to this incident, a person who might have been an undercover agent came to the storehouse and claimed to have a sick father, wanting to join the co-op. The owners had refused and given him names of other businesses and health food stores closer to his home. Not coincidentally, the same man was part of the raid.

According to sources close to the incident, it appears that the incident may have all stemmed from discovery of a bit of noninstitutional beef in a college food-service freezer that was tracked down by a county sanitation official to this same food co-op storehouse. The college's own student food cooperative was widely known for its strident ideological stance about eating organic foods. It seems that the college co-op had joined the well-known food cooperative in order to buy organic foods in bulk from a national organic food distributor, which services buying clubs across the nation. The sanitation official evidently contacted the Department of Agriculture. After the first contact by state officials, the storehouse reportedly wrote the USDA a letter requesting assistance and guidelines for complying with the law. The letter was never answered. Rather, the USDA agent tried several times to infiltrate the co-op, as described above. When his attempts failed, the SWAT team showed up!

According to other sources, "The state Department of Agriculture had been chastised by the courts in several previous instances for its aggression, including trying to entrap an Amish man in a raw milk 'sale,' which backfired when it became known that the Amish believe in a literal interpretation of 'Give to him that asketh thee, and from him that would borrow of thee turn not thou away'" (Matthew 5:42).

The state of Pennsylvania boasts one of the largest Amish populations in the country. Many of the Amish live on acreages where they raise their own food, not unlike the food co-op storehouse, and sell off extra food to neighbors and fellow church members. There is a sense of foreboding that the crackdown on a long-standing, reputable food cooperative could adversely affect the peaceful agrarian way of life not only of the Amish but also of homeschoolers and those families living off the land on rural acreages everywhere. It raises the disturbing possibility that it could become a crime to raise your own food, buy eggs from the farmer down the road, or butcher your own chickens for family and friends—traditional activities that routinely take place in rural America.

Despite growing interest and demand, the freedom to independently produce and purchase food directly from local sources is increasingly under government attack. For those who have food allergies and chemical intolerances or who are on special medical diets, this is becoming a serious health issue. Will Americans retain the right to purchase local and organically produced food from sources they trust?

Happenings such as this are seldom reported by the mainstream American media, but they are becoming more commonplace. If you think that what we have reported might be exaggerated, consider this evidence of an almost identical raid in Southern California posted on YouTube by RTAmerica on August 4, 2010, even as we were writing this essay: www.youtube.com/user/PubliusMMX#p/a/f/o/ifvp3Fxi7Uo

At some point, we've got to start asking some questions about the most prevalent examples of terrorism in this country and begin clearly acknowledging who is terrorizing whom.

What about the Judicial Branch—the Accountability Branch?

Though decisions such as that of the Texas appellate courts in the mass child roundup, the *Printz* case (Tenth Amendment), and a handful of others help even calloused skeptics such as retired attorneys Mancos MacLeod and Mac MacMasterson retain some glimmer of hope for what they call the "so-called" justice system, unfortunately the scales of justice seem to be tipping further and further away from what is right and true. And it's no wonder. Consider the following:

Courts, along with government, share the blame for the unjustifiable abuses that average citizens suffer. It is the job of a judge to be impartial and unbiased, representing blind justice. But many judges have become too secure in their roles and have arrogantly taken on an unbestowed sense of power and importance, believing themselves to be above other citizens and, indeed, above the law.

In this little-known tale of judicial abuse, Judge Sewil had been on the trial court bench for more than twenty years. He had settled in to his position to the point that he was comfortable bending the rules. In one case, he had sentenced a criminal defendant to thirty years to life in prison for sexually abusing a seven-year-old girl. Later, he unilaterally reduced the term and doctored the record following a conversation with the defense attorney after the attorney had written a letter accusing him of interrupting and arguing with her during the sentencing. After Judge

Sewil got the letter, he called the defense attorney to apologize and uni-laterally offered to doctor the record and reduce her client's sentence in exchange for the attorney keeping her mouth shut. Already under scrutiny, Judge Sewil asked the attorney not to mention their *ex parte* conversation or anything else to the prosecutor, and then he secretly changed the record and the sentence.

The judge's duplicity came to light sometime later after the sentenc-ing of a man for poaching a deer. In an overly dramatic sentencing, Judge Sewil asked the defendant if he had ever looked a deer in the eye before he shot it and then launched into a lengthy diatribe about his personal aversion to guns and hunting. When the defendant's brother let out an audible sigh, Judge Sewil ordered court bailiffs to handcuff him and put him in a holding cell until the judge could give him a lengthy lecture on "outbursts" in his courtroom.

This man complained to the Judicial Conduct Commission to no avail, but the timing was bad for Judge Sewil, who was up for reten-tion election. News of both his disrespect and unilateral reduction of the prison sentence became known, and by the time hunters in the state piled on, he didn't stand a chance in the election.

This incident sent a much-needed message to judges everywhere, but how many judges continue to operate under the radar in the same disre-spectful and duplicitous manner? Unfortunately, political and judicial insults are no longer the exception.

The bottom line is that the foundation and core of our country were never designed for the kind of rogue structure that has been built on them, and they have been seriously weakened. The heavy-handedness, intimidation, interference, double-dealing, and abuse *have got to stop!* If any of us tried to do many of the kinds of things our governments are now doing, we would go to prison. If you don't think so, just ask OJ Simpson, Martha Stewart, Jack Abramoff or Bernie Madoff. Don't get us wrong, they should be held fully accountable for their actions. But why shouldn't our governments likewise be held fully accountable?

Chapter 6

What Can We Do about All of This?

We have heard the stories. We have discussed some of the problems. In *Bedrock!* we even imagined some of the possibilities for a better vision and a better future. But where do we go from here? We've been drunk on our federal-dominion port for such a long time. It's time to wake up, shake off the hangover, and get to work. But once the discussion closes, where do we start?

Though it is important to acknowledge where we are, it is even more important to get where we need to go. As Ben Franklin, one of our most-beloved Founding Fathers observed, "Any fool can criticize, condemn, and complain—and most fools do." While we haven't been shy in talking about problems, we aren't interested in merely focusing on complaints. These essays aren't about problems; they're about solutions.

The reason we wrote and published *Bedrock!* first is because it outlines the foundational steps that must be taken to straighten out some of the fundamental issues and problems we face in this country. The discussion in *Bedrock!* focuses on the foundational, personal level. It all starts at the foundation. The only lasting change that will really work is from the bottom up. As we discussed in *Bedrock!*, these core principles include exercising our fundamental freedom of choice—liberty—to exercise personal responsibility, prioritizing production rather than consumption, and learning to live within our means.

Beyond that, as we move from the foundation on up the structure, we need to make some important structural changes to our political system and governments and how they operate.

In 2008, a new president was elected. His election was viewed as a major event that promised change in America. But change is not easily effected. The entire U.S. House of Representatives and one-third of the Senate are up for re-election in 2010—a golden opportunity. Is a big mid-term election the place to start? Many people believe the only way to make a meaningful difference in this country is to start at the top. But as we've said before, we believe *the top* is actually the least important. According to the laws of nature, it is the wrong place to focus most of our efforts and attention because a centralized, top-down approach seldom inures to the long-term benefit of the people.

Nonetheless, we should not pass up the great opportunity we have this year—and will have again in two more years (and two years after that) and during every state and local election in the meantime—to make meaningful changes in the political leadership of our country based on sound fundamental principles. This is a long-term project. It's going to take time to make meaningful changes. We the people need to stand up, take responsibility, and say, "Enough!" And we need to do it over and over again.

As we've said before, it's gotten to the point where we need more than minor tweaks. Actually, we need major structural reforms at every level. We are beyond the point of cosmetic face-lifts. At this point, we have some serious *systemic* issues. Our political system has developed some major structural cracks. These can't be fixed with more spin and superficial Band-Aids. We are in serious need of structural repair.

We must always remember that government is not the foundation; we the people are. With the laws of nature as the bedrock and the Constitution as our tool, we the people are the foundation of this great nation and its very existence. We are the ones who must first honor our proper roles, plant our feet on solid bedrock, and rebuild from there.

What Needs to Change

Here is a list of fundamental, substantive, *structural* reforms for all levels. We're not talking about just putting more Band-Aids on symptoms. We're talking about addressing the core causes and issues at the structural level.

1. Establish clear separation, and restore the appropriate balance of power between the federal government and the states.

What started out as Federalists and evolved into modern Progressives in both parties, along with the media, have made a concerted effort to lead us all to believe that essentially all power, funding, and governmental responsibility must originate in Washington, D.C., when in fact, it does not. In contrast to the freedom enjoyed in this country up to 145 years ago, we the people and the states have become slaves to the federal government.

To that end, the single biggest and most important structural change needed in this country is a restoration of an appropriate balance of power and resources in the relationship between the federal government and the states. It was always intended that there would be checks and balances, including an appropriate balance of power and financial resources (tax revenue) between the federal government and the states.

It has gotten to the point that on one hand the federal government runs roughshod over we the people and the states, and on the other hand, we the people and the states allow it to happen. In many instances, we have now become dependent upon the federal government. To restore a more proper balance, we need to return to a much healthier, arms-length relationship between the states and the federal government. According to the Constitution, there should be a much clearer and cleaner separation than currently exists. Volumes could be written on this subject, but we'll keep it short and simple: all applicable constitutions, federal and state, need to be amended to clarify and strengthen this separation.

As part of that whole equation, and as more fully described in our essay *Prosperity!*, we need to straighten out our governmental financial system. Instead of the federal government collecting taxes and distributing financial aid to the states, taxes should be assessed, collected, and used at the lowest levels possible, with some taxes passed to the federal government for essential federal services as part of a cost-sharing system with the states. Our current system is upside down. But regardless of the details of collection and expenditure of taxes, separation between the federal government and the states, with the states clearly in the proper *parenting* role, needs to happen.

As part of this discussion, we need to return to the earlier discussion in chapter 2 about the proper roles of state and federal governments. That discussion starts with Article 1, Section 8, of the U.S. Constitution. All federal departments, divisions, and agencies that exceed the scope of Article 1, Section 8, need to be eliminated. We must then consider the Tenth Amendment, which expressly provides that any and all powers not specifically delegated to the federal government are reserved to the states and to the people. Although the federal government always attempts to use its twin hammers of the Supremacy Clause and the Commerce Clause to intrude into virtually every aspect of our lives, the bottom line is that the federal government needs to quit acting as though it were a state and stop usurping state powers. To that end, wherever state agencies are in place, any duplicative and overlapping federal regulatory agencies need to be eliminated. In addition to the fact that many federal agencies act in violation of the Tenth Amendment and violate a wide variety of the laws of nature—including inalienable, individual rights—they are a massive waste of financial resources.

The states need to take the lead on this issue. Obviously, Congress has no interest in reining in the federal government, establishing a clearer separation, and yielding to the states on any front. Consequently, the states—remember, the parents of our belligerent federal man-child—must step to the plate and put the federal government in its place. No one else has the constitutional authority or ability to do it. The states must start by taking responsibility for themselves. They must learn how to encourage in-state production, self-sufficiency, and autonomy, and stimulate and perpetuate their own economies. They need to do a much better job of managing their own resources, financial and otherwise, and become net producers. Most important, they need to quit taking money from the federal government.

The states have the ability to initiate and ratify amendments to the Constitution. That's where it's going to have to start. In this regard, we must hold both our state and federal representatives accountable. If they are not committed to sincerely addressing this issue and making something happen, we need to elect people who will.

2. Address the current two-party situation.

As discussed in chapter 4, it is our position that our current two-party *situation* is the single, biggest *obstacle* to meaningful political reform in this country and the kinds of structural reforms we are advocating! That means because of how the two major parties—the Democrat and Republican parties—operate, with their pack mentalities and steadfast refusal to clean up their acts, in a sense they are the single biggest *political* problem we face in America today. How many retiring congressmen have said that the main reason they are getting out is because of all the partisan and party shenanigans and nonsense they have to deal with? Some of these leaders are good people who could do much good in this country, but they are hamstrung by the parties.

Based on such retirements and other recent events, our president recently lambasted the media and others for "stirring up party rancor," asserting that we shouldn't be talking about such things. But the reality is, the parties and politicians themselves need to quit blaming everyone else. The party situation is a serious problem that needs to be talked about. Instead of shutting up about it, we need to address it squarely, tell it like it is, and fix the problem.

As mentioned earlier, according to a renowned political commentator, "There are many men of principle in both parties in America, but there is no party of principle." He also said, "We'd all like to vote for the best man, but he's never a candidate." The bottom line is that the two major political parties and our current two-party system have failed the American people. They are not working for our benefit or for the best interests of this country. The system is broken, and the sooner we make that acknowledgment and start doing something about it, the better off we (and our children, grandchildren and great-grandchildren) are going to be.

At the national level, this single issue must be overcome before many of the other issues can even be addressed. The Founding Fathers knew that a party system wouldn't work. They warned us against it and endeavored against it themselves. It's time for us to do likewise. The good thing about addressing this particular issue is that it does not necessarily depend on our elected lawmakers, who are loath to make any changes that directly affect them and the way they operate. Moreover, it would not absolutely require complicated legislation or any constitutional amendments. Changing the two-party system is entirely up to us. All we need to do is stand up, speak out, and exercise our right to vote.

So what do we do? The best-case scenario would be nonpartisan elections that prioritize principles over personalities. It would be nice if we could snap our fingers and have the parties go away. But the party system seems to be firmly in place.

Although we would prefer to see nonpartisan elections, the reality is that political parties are just tools, and like any tools, they can be used for good or ill. People have and deserve the right to associate as they wish. The issue we have is with the power these two parties have come to wield: the shadow government they operate, the agenda they dictate, and the stranglehold they have on American politics. The media reports that people don't vote. But for all practical purposes, the parties disenfranchise many Americans. The main problem we have with the major political parties in this country is the rogue pack mentality that dominates them as they run amok with a stranglehold on American politics.

The absolute lock the two major parties have on politics has to change. To that end, even a legitimate three-party scenario or an additional umbrella organization for all independent candidates and voices would be a major improvement over the current situation.

It's hard to know the best way to accomplish this. It will require effort, strategy, and time to break the death grip on the system. But as described in the success stories in the next chapter, it is possible. But it will mean that we the people—or at least a significant number of us—will need to wake up and work together. The power to make this change resides entirely with us. Although legislative measures may be helpful, they are not necessary to effect immediate change.

As one statesman said, "Few men change their party for the sake of their principles; many change their principles for the sake of their party." Many elected leaders feel frustrated and trapped by party ties. If you are an elected leader in that situation, we call on you to make a move. Declare independence! Start an independent caucus. If someone else beats you to the punch, join that caucus. Renounce the caucus with your current party and join hands with others who are tired of being abused by party leadership. Don't wait! We need bold leadership, and we need it now! Many Americans stand ready to support you.

It is time to say *no!* It is time to say *Enough!* It is time to take back our power and stop giving the major parties and the media a free pass. It is time to take control of our political arena, our federal government, and our liberty. The American, two-party, political system holds us in chains, but we have the keys. With no more delays, we must actively participate in knowing—and becoming—candidates and rein in the parties by honoring principle over party and not settling for mediocre, media-marketed elected leaders.

Getting Down to Brass Tacks Regarding the Parties

At this point, the single, biggest block of voters in this country now identify themselves as Independents. Most people are fed up with both major parties. Consequently, it is time to vote principles over party and refuse to be boxed into limited choices by biased media coverage. We live in the Information Age. Though the voice of the mainstream media has for decades been the loudest, it needn't continue to be. Mainstream media should become increasingly irrelevant as we the people take control of the discussion and the power. Even when the media ignores good, legitimate candidates, if we will stand up and use the resources and tools at our disposal, we can get the word out and take control over who receives good exposure. We, the independent, freedom-loving people of this country, are the largest voting block. We hold the only real power, but only if we will realize it and utilize it. Without us, all the forceful, controlling entities are nothing. Republicans? Democrats? Many of them are puppets unworthy of our loyalty who wield power over us because we let them.

Many—and particularly Republicans at this point—argue that the only way to fix this problem is by cleaning up the parties—indeed, cleaning up their own party. But history has shown that this doesn't happen. It's not that it can't happen, but despite all the lip service, it hasn't happened. Let's not forget who controls the parties—both major parties. And let's not forget that the Progressive Agenda has completely taken over both major parties. At this point, *fixating* on either one or both of the parties should not be the main objective—it's just another Band-Aid. We need to fix the system. We need to fix the foundation of America's true destiny. And the parties have both proven that they are unreliable tools to accomplish this.

To that end, in addition to persuading existing elected leaders to join our independent cause—regardless of which party they belong to—we need to recruit good, well-qualified, and electable independent and third-party candidates and do what it takes to get them on the ballot and into office. We need to unite our efforts and our votes for liberty-loving, anti-collusion, independent, and minor party candidates and spread the word about them.

The only way this will work is if we the people wake up, stand up, and work together. To that end, we need to create and support a new Independent caucus that serves as an umbrella organization for independents and minor third parties. As long as the major parties remain in control, the minor parties are going to find it extremely difficult to accomplish anything, particularly if they continue splitting independent votes among themselves. But once the stranglehold of the two major parties is broken, making room for more Independents, we can develop a truly pluralistic system with much more healthy political diversity and balance that will be in the best interests of this country—as originally intended. We realize that one of the biggest problems with this approach is legislative committee seniority and leadership, which follows the parties. Consequently, the committee leadership system must likewise be changed. This is something that we the people must insist on.

The basic premises of this Independent caucus need to be the following:

1. It is an umbrella organization that puts principles over party.

2. Anyone—Republican, Democrat, Independent, right, left, or center—can join forces and participate. But we need to throw out labels, which are essentially meaningless and only muddy the waters anyway. We need to stick to principles.

3. Caucus members would join forces to escape and avoid the pack mentality of the two major parties, returning representation to we the people while seeking strength, support, and effectiveness in numbers.

4. The caucus would have few rules—mostly to avoid acting as a mob, and doing what the other parties already do.

5. Ideally, the caucus would have a platform consistent with the basic laws of nature and other universal principles outlined in this and other essays in the *Federalist No. 86* series.

We used to believe it could take years to change the two-party system in such a way that it would make any meaningful difference. But now that we are no longer dependent on elite media; information travels fast—even *independent* information—and our country seems to be awakening to this concept and possibility. At this point, we sincerely believe major changes can happen within just a few election cycles. The membership of the entire U.S. House of Representatives and one-third of the Senate is up for election this year and again in two more years (and two years after that)—not to mention elections at the state and local levels. It's not too late. Even this year, in the elections that have already happened we have already started to make a difference, and in the upcoming general election can continue making an impact and begin laying the foundation for the future.

3. Implement measures to eliminate or reduce professional career politicians.

There are exceptions to every rule, but as a general rule, our governments are run by a pack of professional career politicians who do the bidding of the two major political parties under the direction of big business and the power elite, who direct the affairs of this country. We the people need to retake power. There are some simple steps we should look at to help us with this.

Nomination

For all practical purposes, *nomination* is a very broken concept in our political system. On that score, politicians are already lining up to declare their candidacy for the presidency as well as for governor and congressional races in 2012. This is just plain wrong. *They are campaigning to be nominated, when they should be nominated before they start campaigning.*

As with other needed changes, it may take some time to implement this structural reform, but we the people should choose our leaders rather than allow our leaders to choose themselves. The people who are most eager to be elected to public office are often the most self-interested, self-serving, and potentially abusive of the offices they hope to hold. They are generally people who aspire to become career politicians and be numbered among the ruling elite. As one of our preeminent Founding Fathers said, "Whenever a man has cast a longing eye on public office, a rottenness begins in his conduct." From long, hard experience, we have learned, as our first president exemplified, that one of the first and best qualifications for public office should be that the individual is not bucking for office. Just like George Washington, our leaders should be *called,* nominated by others, and persuaded to accept the nomination for the good of everyone—before they start campaigning!

This also applies to incumbent office holders. They should not think—as many do—that they are entitled to automatic re-nomination. Their hats should not be thrown back in the ring until their constituents have thoroughly measured the fruits of their labors in office and then ask them to serve for another term—followed by further and careful reevaluation.

The bottom line is that candidates and leaders have a completely different mind-set when they are approached, chosen, and persuaded by others to take a turn. When they choose themselves and just throw their hats into the ring, they often have an attitude that it's all about them and they feel accountable only to themselves. But when people are asked to run, they have an entirely different attitude when it comes to accountability.

As long as candidates insist on making self-interested declarations of candidacy, such actions should be viewed as red flags; their true qualifications should be weighed and measured carefully, and dealt with accordingly. Of course, many states need to change their laws regarding declaration for candidacy for this to work; there must be transparency so that the people can see who is self-interested and who isn't. Nomination and support for candidates should be public.

To be nominated, would-be candidates need to be identified based on character, experience, and qualifications. They should be carefully interviewed and vetted, and if found capable and qualified, be recruited to accept a nomination.

In terms of structural reform, in situations that don't require nomination (nonpartisan municipal elections, for example), rather than simply filing papers declaring candidacy, petitions signed by a certain number of unrelated, registered voters, declaring interest should be submitted in order to introduce candidates. The higher the office, the more signatures should be required.

Term Limits

Politicians are like diapers—they both need changing regularly and for the same reason. The premise of this statement is that power corrupts. In a nutshell, over time career politicians tend to become corrupt. The longer they are influenced by money and collusion, the more vulnerable they become to the influence of money and collusion. The evidence is clear—as a general rule, politicians do not become more effective public servants with the passage of time, particularly in terms of representing their constituents, we the people. Even in what might be considered the "best case scenario" the longer elected leaders are in office, the more out of touch they become with reality and with their constituents.

We have known many people who were so disgusted by what they saw in government that they decided to run for office so that they could straighten things out and make a change. But with few exceptions, and despite their best intentions, they become products of the system and lose the ideals they started with.

It has been demonstrated that the longer people serve in elected office, the less transparent their behavior becomes and the less concerned they become about complying with open and public meeting laws. They begin to see themselves as above the law—both the laws of man *and* the laws of nature, both as individuals *and* as they operate as a body of elected lawmakers. The longer it goes, the worse it gets and the harder it is for somebody new to come in and make changes.

The concept of six-year terms for senators without term limits and lifetime appointment of judges was straight out of the original Federalists' elitist, aristocratic playbook. Then as now, the wealthy elite wanted to control and hang on to power as long as possible. But two hundred years later, what credible argument can be made in support of this structure? Especially, if senators aren't appointed by the states, as originally intended, and getting elected is mostly just a very expensive popularity contest, that often goes to the candidate with the deepest pockets, regardless of actual qualifications.

The two-party situation and term limits go hand in hand, and changing them both is the biggest thing we can do to reform and take back politics in this country—at all levels. We believe that most problematic political issues would resolve themselves if we could simply get away from perpetuating the careers of professional politicians and the ruling elite who have taken over this country through the two-party system and the corruption that goes along with it.

One past U.S. president said, "One thing our Founding Fathers could not foresee . . . was a nation governed by professional politicians who had a vested interest in getting reelected. . . . They probably envisioned a fellow serving a couple of hitches and then looking . . . forward to getting back to the farm."

That is the way it should be. Today, career politicians acting hand in hand with the two major political parties make up the most critically needed change in our political system.

Unfortunately, elected lawmakers and politicians have clearly demonstrated their opposition to all such measures—essentially any measures that regulate how *they* behave and do business. During the 1990s, twenty states adopted some form of term limits, primarily via citizen initiatives. After relentless attack by state legislatures and in the court system, however, only about five actually retained their measures. In Louisiana, by far the best example of what can and should be done, the people succeeded in adopting and passing a state constitutional amendment imposing term limits. That needs to happen in all states and at the federal level. If Louisiana can do it, so can the rest of the country. A constitutional amendment needs to be advanced to accomplish such objectives at the national level.

Along with the two-party stranglehold, the ruling elite, with its professional, career politicians and four-, five-, and six-term senators, simply have to go. With lengthy terms and the revolving door between politicians and lobbyists both removed, collusion between the public and private sectors would be drastically reduced.

These limitations need to apply to our justice system as well. Too many judges stay in office far too long. For most judicial offices, terms should not be more than about twelve years. Lifetime appointments to the federal bench are utter nonsense. Even for the U.S. Supreme Court, terms of service should be twenty years at most. If all our laws were based on the fundamental principles of the laws of nature and on the Constitution, we wouldn't need to create artificial continuity by trying to have a judge on the bench for thirty to forty years just to bring some degree of stability to the equation. Remember the laws of nature: if people don't have to produce because they have a guaranteed slot for life, odds are they won't produce!

A Part-time Legislature

Another good idea to help rein in Congress, end career politics, and reduce excessive federal spending would be to eliminate the full-time Congress. This is not a new idea, but it is a good one. Those who think that Congress needs to be in session almost all year or that having a full-time Congress is in the best interests of the American people are kidding themselves. Congress spends vast amounts of time and resources justifying its actions, the majority of which exceed constitutional bounds. Clearly, Congress causes more problems than it prevents or solves. We would all be better off if Congress were in session not more than six months a year. And to take things a step farther in the right direction, we should take a page from the Texas Constitution and have Congress meet only every other year. Members of Congress and their staffs should be paid accordingly—approximately 25 percent of their current salaries. This would essentially eliminate any financial incentive to make a professional career out of elected politics and return our elected leaders to the role of *citizen lawmakers*.

The only congressional session held every two years should be held during the six months immediately preceding each congressional election. This would require that members of Congress focus more on *governing* and the truly important matters at hand and less on campaigning. By limiting the amount of time in session, they would be forced to focus on the *real* issues and have less time to engage in the mischief they do now, which results in wasted time, effort, and money as well as ridiculous thousand- and two-thousand page bills. Also, if legislative sessions were held immediately prior to elections, the fruits of congressional labors would be fresh in people's minds at the general election every other year. As someone once said, "When an election is coming, universal peace is declared and the foxes have a sincere interest in prolonging the lives of the poultry."

Such provisions would eliminate the profession of career politician by forcing elected officials to have a real job at least half the time. It would also encourage them to spend more time in their districts, talking and *listening* to their constituents. Because time spent in session would be a premium, lawmakers would focus on true policy priorities rather than on the unproductive and expensive nonsense they pursue in the current system. And finally, this could result in significant cost savings in a number of different ways. In addition to reducing congressional and staff salaries, it would reduce the amount of time legislators have to creatively spend taxpayer money in the fourth branch of government.

Again, the only way this will ever happen is through citizen legislation or constitutional amendment. As in almost all areas, our lawmakers have demonstrated their unwillingness to exercise responsibility when it comes to governing themselves. As a well-known statesman once said, "I have come to the conclusion that politics is too serious a matter to leave the politicians entirely to their own devices."

4. Insist on better qualified candidates for public office.

Again, like the party situation, this is a fundamental structural reform that doesn't require complicated legislation. It's entirely up to us! If, as our friend Worth says, it really is "90 percent of politicians who give the rest a bad name," we need to figure out what it takes to be that rare individual who is well qualified for public office (and you can't figure that out by looking at our current politicians), and do everything in our power to get them in office—lots of them. As has been said, "It is not in the nature of politics that the best men should be elected; the best men generally do not want to govern their fellow men."

So on one hand, this seems like a tough issue. On the other hand, just like the laws of nature, it's really rather simple. At first, we, as Publius MMX—a group of recovering Federalists—couldn't agree among ourselves exactly what the basic qualifications should be. But one thing we agree upon is the number of elected officials we see who have no experience in the private sector or *real life*. We're looking for those who have a genuine understanding of and know how to apply the laws of nature in government. Many politicians have essentially no idea what the real world is all about. They have had no experience in what it takes to make payroll, stay in business, make sound executive-level decisions, or stay within budget.

We don't speak on this lightly. Based on our experience, we see career politics as a major *dis*qualification because as a general rule, politicians don't get better with time. Frankly, based on our experience, we are unimpressed with fancy resumes filled with public sector experience; we much prefer more real-life grit. We can't even begin to understand the media's infatuation with such candidates and its determination to shamelessly promote them at the expense of much better-qualified though perhaps less charismatic candidates. Elected leaders should have a firm grasp of what it is like to live and operate under the rules, regulations, and laws that our governments are imposing on us.

Recently we were listening to a major national radio program that has a lot of objective credibility. The host and other commentators were discussing current congressional candidates and races in a number of states. Not once in the whole discussion did they mention anything about the candidates' policy positions, principles, platform, judgment, or any of the other factors that should lead the list of qualifications for public office. The one and only thing they talked about was campaign coffers and which candidates were leading in fundraising—as if that were the highest and most important qualification for office. This example provides a pretty good idea of just how messed up our political system is.

Although we don't want to get lost in personal details in this section, Mancos MacLeod—another retired lawyer with time on his hands—probably would not be our first choice as a candidate for elected office. Matt James, on the other hand, whose entire occupational background has been in the private sector, along with a term on a city council, might be a real good choice. Rosie McLayne, the proactive paralegal, might be another good choice.

But perhaps the best choice of all might be Nick Romero. We'll talk more about him in the next chapter, but Nick is the father of five children ages three to seventeen. He was seriously injured in an industrial accident and left permanently disabled. To help support the family, his wife went back to school to become a nurse, working part time. Money was tight. They lived in a modest rental house on a small lot. But they lived as frugally and self-sufficiently as possible. Nick doesn't have a lot of formal education, but he does have a degree in real life and from the school of hard knocks. He knows how to produce, how to budget, and how to live within his means. He knows how to say no. He knows how to think and has learned to speak in public. He also knows how to stand up and take action, and he has done so. Most important, Nick possesses sound judgment. He has good fruit to show for his labors. There is every reason to believe he would make a good elected leader, and he may be better qualified than any of us.

A fundamental principle that applies to qualifications for office is "by their fruits ye shall know them." We need to quit paying so much attention to what politicians and candidates look like and tell us and look more closely at what they do. We need to look very closely at their actions and the fruits of their labors. Have they stood on their own two feet long enough to learn some lessons of life? Do they know how to live within their means? Do they know what it means to produce? If all they have is talk, maybe we ought to look elsewhere for our leaders. Once we have seen their fruits and determined that they are good, then we will have more confidence in putting greater responsibility upon them.

At the end of the day, the decisions rest with we the people. As we wake up, stand up, and start taking back our government, we'll be a lot more particular about the people we elect to public office. Let's raise the bar. Let's elect leaders who possess sound judgment. In addition to meeting applicable age or citizenship requirements, we believe that qualified candidates should possess all—or at least a majority—of the following:

- A strong commitment to the concept that the single, highest priority and paramount purpose of government at all levels is to protect individual, inalienable rights based on the laws of nature.

- A fundamental understanding of the laws of nature and the importance of personal responsibility, along with a commitment to apply such principles.

- A solid understanding of the Constitution of the United States and of the constitution of any individual state they serve, including a belief in properly balanced government and a commitment to abide by constitutional principles.

- A commitment to preserve liberty by making government—at all levels—more transparent and accountable to the people and a demonstrated willingness to defend and protect the inalienable rights of individuals, including life, liberty, and property.

- A determination to hold the body in which they serve, and any others over which they have oversight, financially accountable by balancing applicable budgets, with no allowances for financing of general government obligations and operations through debt.

- A willingness to declare all conflicts of interest and not participate in any votes or discussions involving any entity from which they, their immediate families, or any business interests receive any direct benefit (including large campaign contributions, gifts, and so forth).

- A commitment to seek to limit government and to maintain a proper balance among the levels and branches of government.

- A commitment to reduce and simplify new legislation, recognizing that we already have an overabundance of unnecessary laws.

- A commitment to prioritize principles over party and politics.

Upstanding candidates for public office should be willing to make such commitments and abide by them, even after they are elected and exposed to all the corrupting influences that seem to overwhelm elected leaders and the *system* they operate in. If, after being elected, individuals demonstrate that they are unable or unwilling to keep these commitments, they should not be reelected.

5. Eliminate collusion between the public and private sectors.

We address some aspects of this issue in *Prosperity!*, including certain aspects of inappropriate collusion and competition between government and business. Here, we wish to address the inappropriate relationships that often exist between elected officials and lobbyists and the media.

Disclosure and Accountability for Conflicts of Interest

Lawmakers and government officials—at all levels and in all branches of government—should be prohibited from voting on, discussing, or deciding any issue in which they have direct conflicts of interest based on any direct benefits to themselves, their families, and their business interests, or based on campaign contributions or lobbying efforts that go beyond a reasonable assigned cumulative value. Period. This standard should be a no-brainer, but violations occur all the time.

It's not just Washington D.C. where this happens. The latest example we are personally aware of (that otherwise flew completely under the radar) involved a state legislative matter just this year, in 2010, in which it was in the best interests of one special interest group if certain legislation did not emerge from committee by a certain date. In exchange for large campaign contributions to the committee chairman, and even larger payments to two separate lobbyists, the delay was arranged—simply and easily. Similar examples are a dime a dozen in city halls and on capitol hills throughout this country. But the automatic result of these contributions should have been the declaration of a conflict of interests that would have prohibited the committee chairman from having any further involvement in the discussion or related decisions. But, of course, if that had been the case, the contributions would not have been made in the first place, which is exactly the point.

The credo should be: Lend your support if you can, but your money will not buy you political influence.

However, because lawmakers have demonstrated their steadfast refusal to regulate their behavior and how they operate, we the people need to have an increased ability to hold them accountable and subject them to prosecution—either by applicable attorneys general or as private citizens under the private attorney general doctrine. Under private attorney general doctrine, if the state attorney general is too busy and/or refuses to act on an allegation of public corruption, a private citizen can initiate action. If the citizen's case prevails in the court system, under the private attorney general doctrine, he or she is entitled to recover attorneys fees to make it worth the while. If lawmakers are found guilty, they should be subject to a range of penalties, including impeachment and damages. They need to be held accountable for selfish and unethical behavior. Enough already! And they need to have more than just a slap on the wrists. To raise the bar, and prevent frivolous actions, however, losers should be required to pay attorneys' fees and court costs. Again, there is no way we can reasonably expect the fox to do an acceptable job of guarding the henhouse.

Relationship with the Media

Unlike in the past, when the media—particularly the press—at least pretended to take a neutral, objective approach to government affairs, the media has now become the fifth branch of government and aggressively advances its own political agenda. And, just as the government itself, the media does its best to determine winners and losers. It gives those it chooses as winners as much positive play as possible and ignores or castigates those it attempts to make losers. The presidential race of 2008 was a prime example of this. Although President Obama had a sizeable funding advantage, he didn't really need the financial advantage. He got so much free positive publicity from the media that the funding disparity was largely irrelevant. The same applies to a wide variety of other issues. What we get is the media's spin, based on its agenda.

What do we do about this? We don't claim to have a lot of good answers. The last thing we really need is a media czar or more regulations. Free speech and freedom of the press are fundamental inalienable rights. More than anything, we the people need to *wake up to this reality* and vote with our pocketbooks and our viewership. We need to quit patronizing media outlets that cannot be trusted to give us a straight scoop and both sides of the story without being tainted by their own philosophical agendas. Eventually, the media marketplace will probably straighten some of this out. In the meantime, we need to be careful about what we believe based on what we see, hear, and read.

6. Implement campaign finance reform.

It has been said, "Politics is the gentle art of getting votes from the poor and campaign funds from the rich by promising to protect each from the other."

Campaign finance reform is a cloudy, divisive issue with a lot of big money, powerful entities, and career politicians trying to control the rules in order to benefit their own self-interests over others. We don't claim to have all the answers in this regard either, but we do know two things. Based on the laws of nature, power and money have a natural tendency to corrupt. Elected offices in this country should not be for sale. As one of our preeminent Founding Fathers said, "Few men have virtue enough to withstand the highest bidder."

In addition to money and finance, this whole issue has become clouded and confused by the injection of the discussion of "corporate free speech." To that end, let's not forget that inalienable, natural rights were bestowed by the laws of nature—before governments even existed and before artificial, man-made creations such as corporations, unions, PACS, and political parties existed. How can artificial, man-made creations be entitled to free-speech protection on the basis that they have inalienable rights? It's like saying that inalienable property rights come from zoning ordinances. It flies in the face of reason and turns the concept of inalienable rights based on the laws of nature on its head.

There is no question that campaign financing has gotten out of control and that reform is needed. So we ask ourselves a series of questions:

How can we reduce or eliminate the conflict "corporate free speech" is causing? What can be done about politicians unfairly supporting one business, corporation, union, or state over another? What can be done about special interest groups getting involved in elections where they have no interest other than to buy votes? How do we get things back to we the people and away from corporations and unions?

The bottom line is that there is no need for complicated legislation. The best way to deal with campaign finance reform is by addressing conflicts of interest as outlined above and confronting the current buying and selling of elected offices with the following list of simple rules.

Think about what would happen to the system if power were returned to us, the people, and if the following rules were implemented:

1. Restrict campaign contributions to individual contributions only—no corporate, business, union, party, or PAC contributions.

2. Eliminate contributions from outside a candidate's own district or the area the candidate is elected to serve, including foreign contributions.

3. Restrict contributions to political parties and PACs to individuals only—no corporate, business, unions, or PAC contributions.

4. Limit the contribution amount per individual to a party, PAC, and candidate to a reasonable amount (say $1,000 for local elections, $2,500 for state elections, and $5,000 for congressional and presidential elections).

Although these rules would obviously provoke a lot of kicking and screaming from the major political parties, big business, unions, and career politicians, they would go a long way toward cleaning up the current mess.

With respect to rule 1, with corporate, union, and party contributions and financial incentives out of the picture and party financing drastically reduced, representation would be brought back to the people. Representatives should represent the people who elect them and whom they are intended to serve rather than be subservient to corporate deal making. Instead of kowtowing to high-dollar special interests, public servants should work for their constituents.

Just as George Washington noted that political parties bring extraordinary, *unnatural* force to the equation, with power to fractionalize and unduly manipulate the political process, so can and do other manmade creations, including corporations, unions, and businesses. Corporations, unions, businesses, PACs, and political parties do not elect our leaders; we the people do! There is a reason for that. As we have discussed before, we should *not* have a government "of the party, by the party, for the party." Likewise, we should not have a government "of the union, by the union, for the union" or "of the corporation, by the corporation, for the corporation." We need a government "*of the people, by the people, for the people.*"

With respect to rule 2, elected representatives would be allowed to represent the people they are elected to serve rather than be beholden to outside interests and subservient to deals made with lobbyists who are only trying to buy votes and don't care where they come from. Instead of kowtowing to interests outside their jurisdiction, public servants could focus their efforts on working for their own constituents, whom they have been elected to represent.

With respect to rule 3, such a provision would naturally and specifically help return representation and accountability to we the people, not to the party or its bosses. This would go a long way toward reducing the dangerous mob mentality that persuades politicians to listen more to their parties and party bosses than to their own constituents.

Finally, with respect to rule 4, rather than candidates being beholden to a few people with greater access and resources, they would, of necessity, be supported by and accountable to the masses, including the rich, the middle class, and the poor alike.

Because power and money have a tendency to corrupt, current laws naturally force national and state officials running for office to do what special interests want regardless of what we the people need.

7. Drastically reduce the fourth branch of government.

Under the direction of major political parties and big corporations, massive bureaucracies run this country, with complicity from our Congress. The end result is a nation that is very different than the one intended and designed by its founders. Even our most ardent Federalist forefathers would undoubtedly roll over in their graves if they could see what has happened. The current state of the fourth, administrative branch has mutated and multiplied government far beyond anything they ever could have imagined or would have approved.

As we've stated in both this essay and in *Prosperity!*, the fourth branch of government is out of control. In today's world, if government isn't competing with private business, it's regulating it to death. The fourth branch, with all its parasitic agencies, needs to be pared down to size. One of the first places to start is by eliminating all duplication among agencies—in both federal and state governments. When government starts adhering to the laws of nature, allows individuals to take personal responsibility, and quits acting as a nanny state, the fourth branch of government can be reduced to a fraction of its current size, with spending reduced correspondingly.

One of the best and simplest ways to do this is to quit funding most activities of the fourth branch of government. Most government bureaucrats do what they do for one reason and one reason only—because they are funded to do so. They don't do things they are not paid and not funded to do. As we discussed in *Bedrock!*, when there is no equity in a home, the owner has little incentive to hang on. It's natural because there is no value to fight for. On the same basis, and in accordance with the laws of nature, the simplest way to deal with many of the abuses and excesses we see in government is to simply stop funding them. If there were no financial incentives to further grow the empire, nature would take its course. There would be a corresponding double bottom line: life would be better and we would start digging our way out of the hole we're in. This would kill two birds with one stone: the fourth branch of government would be pared down to size, and we would save *a lot* of money in the process.

8. Reform the legal system.

Although much more can be written to address issues in the justice/legal system than can be presented here, we cannot ignore it altogether. Aside from the right to a jury trial and a presumption of innocence, the workings of much of our legal system are the product of an elitist fantasy, made mostly for the benefit of lawyers. Lifetime appointment of federal judges is an aristocratic dream. But even worse than lifetime appointment of federal judges is the fact that in many states, judges are chosen by popular election—especially partisan elections—rather than by appointment. Having to stand for election turns judges into politicians, with all the issues and problems that go along with that designation. How can we reasonably expect fairness and impartiality when the deciding criteria are essentially based on popularity and financial resources?

It's not a judge's job to make law; it's a judge's job to interpret and apply it, handing down decisions in the justice system impartially, as if blindfolded. But having been around the block as we have, we've had ample opportunity to see just how much a role the hand of politics plays in the system. Since virtually all judges are lawyers, how will they treat other lawyers who run against them? How will they treat big campaign contributors? What is their attitude likely to be toward corporations, unions, or individuals who campaign against them? Clearly, this needs to change. This should be a no-brainer, especially now that the U.S. Supreme Court has undone a good share of a century's worth of campaign finance reform based on one small element of the issue—holding that the corporate right of free speech is on par with individual, inalienable rights and, therefore, entitled to constitutional protection. When it comes to judicial elections, one very credible and experienced judge has said, "Trying to ignore special interests in elections, especially judicial elections, is like trying to ignore an alligator in your bathtub."

Some states have a system in which judges are appointed by the governor from a short list of well-qualified nominees who are vetted and whose names are submitted by a qualified nominating committee, who are then confirmed by the state senate, and who are subject to regular *retention* elections. Every state might want to look at this process as a way to help clean up the judicial system in this country. We need to get back to the fundamental concept of blind or impartial justice.

But judges aren't the only challenge in the justice system. Japan trains one attorney for every nine engineers; in America, those numbers are reversed. Attorneys are in great supply and work hard to justify their existence by drumming up and stretching out ridiculous and unnecessary litigation. Attorneys and their infatuation with pursuing petty lawsuits are one of a host of parasites on our nation. Perhaps the only parasite that sucks more lifeblood out of our nation than the legal system is the fourth branch of government. In states where judges are elected, inane tort awards have become prevalent. New guidelines are needed that will punish unnecessary litigation through loser-pay penalties for unreasonable suits. Regardless of how this is handled, it should be handled by the states. This means that if some states insist on continuing to have a corrupt state judicial system, that's their call; they should be the masters of their own destinies in this area.

This just scratches the tip of the iceberg regarding needed reforms in the justice/legal system. We'll save the rest of the discussion for another day.

9. Implement nullification, referenda, and recall elections.

Although we, like the Founding Fathers, firmly believe in a constitutional republic, we also believe there is a proper role and place for us—we the people and the individual states—to hold our elected representatives accountable when they go too far, spend too much, or act contrary to the will of the people and the best interests of our nation. Based on our experience, we can clearly see that sometimes our elected leaders need help governing themselves. Consequently, under some circumstances and in accordance with constitutional measures, we believe that someone other than our elected lawmakers should be entitled to vote on what they do and how they conduct their business—*our* business—in order to protect and defend inalienable, individual rights. That is the fundamental premise behind ratification, nullification, referenda, citizens' legislation and other tools and means by which the states and *the people* have a chance to approve what our elected leaders—at all levels—have done in matters of particular importance. These tools are a fundamental measuring stick and a legitimate means of holding our elected leaders accountable for their actions. We believe ratification, as described in the discussion on constitutional amendments below, is a tool that should be put in place for much more frequent use regarding congressional legislation.

Moreover, we believe that many of our elected lawmakers repeatedly demonstrate a lack of will or ability to adequately govern themselves. Just like the rattlesnake in the story in chapter 4, they are what they are and simply can't or won't behave otherwise. Therefore, under certain circumstances, we the people—the electorate, the constituents—need to have the tools to be able to step in and do something when our elected lawmakers refuse to do what is needed.

We know that direct citizen legislation, including initiatives and referenda, stick in the craw of many conservatives, who are concerned (just as we are) about mob-rule democracy. But given the current state of things, particularly when it comes to how our elected leaders operate and conduct *our* business, and spend our money, it's the fox guarding the henhouse. Who is watching the foxes who are guarding the henhouse, and holding them accountable? Consequently, we believe that additional tools need to be available to effectively address these issues. With so many career politicians calling the shots, simply electing new and different representatives is not always a viable and effective solution.

Because of the collusion that occurs between big business and the legislative and executive branches, we need these tools. Many laws are now passed that are not in the best interests of the American people. Therefore, when ill-advised laws, including out-of-control spending packages, are passed, voters should have a right and a mechanism to veto such legislation.

If we are unsuccessful even after doing everything we have listed to correct course, including breaking the death grip the current two-party system has on our nation and working to elect well-qualified leaders who voluntarily commit to term limits and other reforms, we've still got to be able to close the deal. If, despite everything else we have done, our lawmakers still fail to enact laws to hold themselves accountable, we the people need to have the tools to hold them accountable ourselves.

To that end, all state and the federal governments need provisions for the exercise of citizen initiatives and referenda under the right circumstances. We agree that citizen-initiative legislation has gotten out of control in some places, including California. But under certain, well-defined circumstances, particularly when it comes to vetoing unacceptable laws and enacting laws governing how our elected leaders conduct business, we believe we have reached a point in this country where the tool of citizens' legislation, including initiatives and referenda has become a necessity.

Think about it. What evidence is there that our elected leaders have the collective will to regulate themselves and the way they conduct business? When it comes to how they do business, under the dictates and direction of big business and the major parties, they are much more interested in doing what is in *their* best interests and the best interests of those who give them direction instead of doing what is in *our* best interest. Consequently, as discussed below, all state and federal constitutions should be amended to provide such tools of accountability.

Having said that, we have our own axes to grind with much of the citizen legislation we have seen in recent years. Much of it is overly complicated and poorly written. If initiative legislation becomes prolific, it loses its effectiveness. It soon has the same effect as the boy who cried "wolf" a few times too many. Consequently, we believe this legislative method should be primarily reserved for situations involving matters of substantial consequence, when the people are otherwise powerless against their lawmakers—situations such as now.

Due to partnerships that exist between big business and the legislative and executive branches, there is little chance for many enacted laws to truly be in the best interests of the American people. Therefore, when a bad law is passed, voters should have a right to veto that law by referendum. Just the possibility of this alone would help hold lawmakers much more accountable and cause them to behave more responsibly. When our elected leaders vote for things such as sweeping, ill-advised health care reform and massive federal bailouts, such legislation should be subject to referendum and possible rejection by the people who are the ones who have to pay the bill.

This just makes sense. When local governments want to spend money above their budget and normal tax revenue, they have to hold a bond election. General obligation requires general consent. Why can't that be required at the federal level as most of the states and cities do and as was recently done in Iceland? Why shouldn't we the people be able to vote on general financial obligations, particularly those that benefit only certain, limited-interest groups?

One argument against this is that our federal government moves so slowly. But over the course of the past several years, we have seen government move at breathtaking speed, spending dollars so fast it makes our heads spin, in numbers and terms so large they no longer have any relevance. What's a billion? What's a trillion? What's a quadrillion? And what's the problem with that? *It's money our government doesn't have and money that our children, grandchildren, and great-grandchildren will have to come up with to pay the bills.*

After massive spending increases the past two years and at a time when our national GDP has been flat, government spending is projected to continue increasing at a rate of almost 10 percent a year for the next several years. Meanwhile, in 2008, the average household income in the United States was estimated at $50,303, a 3.6 percent drop from 2007. It is expected that 2009 and 2010 will show even bigger drops in income. Obviously, government spending and personal income are going in opposite directions. Instead of speeding up the spending process, we need to slow it down. If our financial system and our major industries are so fragile that they might collapse just because we take the time to make a careful decision, it shows just how vulnerable we have become as a country. We need to start making fundamental structural changes. We need to start talking about something beyond temporary Band-Aids funded by more spending!

Because we are at the mercy of our elected representatives, we the people of the United States should also have the option of recall elections. Some states already have this, but it needs to be available in every state and at every level, including the federal government. When elected officials completely lose sight of their rightful limitations, we should have the ability to remove them without having to wait for their next election cycle, which could be as many as four to five years down the road, depending on the office. If they are too caught up in themselves to voluntarily step down, we should have the option to meet reasonably rigorous requirements to remove them from office.

Increased accountability from elected officials to those they serve would be a natural and positive consequence of the availability of this tool. If all elected officials were subject to recall elections, they would be encouraged to listen to their constituents from day to day instead of just during an election season.

In conclusion, we believe there is a need for well-written citizen legislation, particularly regarding referenda and spending bills, as well as initiatives regarding political ethics reform. While most of the necessary changes should be incorporated into constitutions by amendment, we've got to be able to close the deal. Although there is no provision for direct citizen legislation in the Constitution, our history makes it clear that elected officials need help governing themselves. Citizens need a route around the party roadblock and career politicians. As long as the federal government is going to try to act as if it were a state and usurp states' rights, Congress should be subject to the same limitations and accountability that state legislators are. It's time to say *Enough!* and have available citizen-led options and tools for regaining control.

10. Pass constitutional amendments.

With this part of the discussion, we are bringing the Federalist / Anti-Federalist debate full circle. At this point, 220 years later, it is difficult for a bunch of recovering Federalists who have fully enjoyed the high life of federal dominion to admit that the Anti-Federalists may have been right about a good many things—and not just about the need for the Bill of Rights to project inalienable rights. Though we agree with all who say we must do a much better job of adhering to the Constitution and cease treating it as irrelevant, by the time you have read this far, it should come as no surprise that we believe the Constitution needs to be amended in some important ways.

We know we're going to catch heat from some quarters for even suggesting that the Constitution be amended. The question will inevitably be asked, "If the Constitution was divinely inspired in the first place and has served us well up to this point, why should it be changed now?" We have 220 years of experience by which to measure the Constitution's performance—not as theory but as practical application. On the other hand, we have seen the Constitution amended for such passing fancies as Prohibition (and then amended again to repeal it) as well as for other such shallow issues. The Founders knew that issues and circumstances would arise that would require changes and amendments. That is why they specifically provided not just one means but two to make needed changes. The important thing they expected of us is that we make any such amendments in accordance with the rule of law and the laws of nature, always remembering that this country was intended to be a constitutional republic.

When we engage in this exercise, we believe that we all need to be at least somewhat intellectually honest with ourselves. Although the Constitution prescribes governmental structures we still abide by to a large extent, the reality is that many provisions of the Constitution, such as the separation of powers and checks and balances, have been consistently ignored for years. For all practical purposes, it's as though the Constitution has been gradually changed by perpetual creeping, unwritten amendment, and by the courts. In fact, in some people's minds it has been amended in practice and application to the point that it has become largely irrelevant.

What we have is a Constitution that embodies the original Federalist agenda, with a Bill of Rights included in the first ten amendments as essentially the only bone thrown to the Anti-Federalists and their arguments and concerns. As the Federalist/Progressive agenda has mutated, morphed, multiplied, and gained strength and momentum over the years, the weak checks and balances and separation of powers outlined in the Constitution have proven wholly inadequate to the task of keeping the Federalist/Progressive agenda and the federal government in check. In fact, our federal government has become exactly what the Anti-Federalists feared—or worse. The Federalist/Progressive agenda has become so powerful that it overwhelms the original checks and balances as well as much of the original intent of the Constitution.

We believe that we all owe ourselves enough intellectual honesty to address the reality of the situation instead of engaging in theoretical discussions and assertions about what might have been had we actually followed the Constitution. What we have done in this country is to allow the original Federalist agenda to grow almost completely unchecked to the point that it is so far out of control that the governments we have today are barely recognizable compared to the governments we believe our Founders intended through the Constitution.

We can study our history and see both the strengths and the weaknesses in our primary governing document. When we undertake such study, we will see that vast, unconstitutional bureaucracies have been built that even the original Federalists would find repulsive. We the people, acting in accordance with the laws of nature, are the foundation. And we the people, in order to form a more perfect union, need to establish additional protections in order to see that the fourth branch of government is dismantled and, for the sake of our children and grandchildren, never rebuilt.

We need to put protections in place to ensure that political parties and self-serving elites can no longer rule for decades at a time. Government, laws, and the Constitution are only *tools* for governing. In the end, any tool can be used for good or bad. The Constitution and the Declaration of Independence are fundamental tools for our republic and, indeed, certain aspects of the Constitution should never be changed. Those provisions, based on the laws of nature and nature's God, that protect inalienable and self-evident natural rights—including life, liberty, and property—should never be allowed to pale or be amended. But it is time to get our government working for the people again. No more should we allow the elite in this country to use the tool of government to attack us.

As noted in our other essays, including *Prosperity!*, we sincerely assert that the Constitution is in need of amendment in several important ways. In addition to a balanced budget amendment, which many people support, we believe there is a need for government finance-related amendments, as outlined in *Prosperity!* We also believe there is a serious need for several other amendments to help restore an appropriate balance of power between the federal government and the states, including clarification of the scope and application of the Tenth and Fourteenth Amendments as well as the Commerce Clause and the Establishment Clause.

And let's not forget that whatever we do, including anything initiated or passed by Congress, must be ratified by at least two-thirds of the states. So we might just as well do something that will help restore some reasonable balance of power. To that end, we believe the Seventeenth Amendment should be repealed so that senators are once again appointed by state legislators to represent and protect state interests.

And while we're at it, we believe in additional amendments that would provide such changes as term limits to help end the cycle of professional, career politicians; provisions for direct citizen legislation, particularly referenda to veto excessive government spending and initiatives governing lawmakers and how *they* behave and conduct *our* business; and provisions addressing the fourth branch of government as well as our judicial system. In fact, we believe the constitutions of all fifty states should likewise be amended.

But one of the single most useful constitutional amendments would employ and expand the concept and scope of *ratification,* or nullification. This would be a much-needed check on the federal government and on federal legislation. Instead of being reserved solely for constitutional amendments initiated by Congress, provision should be made so that whenever Congress passes major legislative initiatives that might be unacceptable to we the people and the states, there would be a process for taking a preliminary state vote—by state governors. Any state could initiate this process. If 60 percent of state governors voted in favor of a ratification/nullification election, then the legislative initiative would be suspended until it was put to a vote by state legislatures. At that point, to become effective the legislation would have to be ratified by state legislatures, requiring a two-thirds majority vote. This would give the states the power to veto abusive and unacceptable federal legislation. The federal government should be precluded from being involved in or funding this process, and it should likewise be precluded from lobbying or campaigning for or against passage.

The Constitution was made to be amended. Over the course of the past 220 years, it has been amended successfully on eighteen different occasions with twenty-seven different amendments. It is not an easy process; nor should it be because amending the Constitution should not be considered lightly. Over the course of the past two centuries, eleven thousand amendments have been proposed, but only twenty-seven have stuck. The bigger our country has become, the harder it has become to change the Constitution.

Amending the Constitution is a two-part process that can be started by either a two-thirds majority of both houses of Congress or by two-thirds of the states through their state legislatures. In either case, to take effect, an amendment must be ratified—approved and accepted—by three-fourths of the states. The problem with both of these routes is that they require action by politicians—politicians who no longer act in the best interests of the people. This is why we need a major overhaul.

The constitutional amendments we advocate have to do with how all governments—federal, state, and local—govern themselves and conduct business. Our elected lawmakers have proven that they are ineffective at governing themselves in the process of governing the rest of us. Many are reelected and are even popular, but the vast majority have a poor track record when it comes to serving the people.

No matter how many people vote otherwise, tyranny of the majority over the minority should never be allowed to infringe on inalienable rights that existed long before the laws of man.

Obviously, this is something the states will have to initiate and pursue. Although Congress has the authority, it has no incentive. The status quo serves the federal government's purposes well. As feeble as the Constitution has become in practice in many respects, particularly in terms of protecting states' rights, the states still have the power and authority to change it—to rein in the federal government, turn things around, correct course, and get this country back on track. This is something the states must do before the federal government takes us over the edge—and we're getting close.

As Amended

Chapter 7

Stories about People who have Walked the Walk—
Making a Difference for Good

We realize that sometimes there is a big gap between theory and reality. So we have sought out real-life stories about people who are doing more than just talking the talk—they're walking the walk. People who have stood up, gotten involved, applied principles discussed here, and thus made significant and positive differences for the good of this country, both to help fix the foundation, and fulfill its ultimate divine destiny.

Local Zoning Ordinance Challenge Revisited

In our first story, we return to the ambitious Rosie McLayne and her neighbors and their efforts to take on their town's new zoning ordinance. When we left Rosie's story, the town council had just adopted an incomprehensible one hundred-page, one-size-fits-all zoning and land-use ordinance. The ordinance removed rights from property owners and limited use of their land to those things specifically permitted in the ordinance. Some people in Rosie's small town, including the mayor and two council members, thought this was a major step in the right direction. The measures were going to help clean up this little agricultural community. Among other things, they would *regulate* home businesses and push all livestock and dirty, stinking agriculture out of town. The measures were intended to drag the town, kicking and screaming if necessary, into the 21st century.

In rural communities across the country many such ordinances have been adopted over recent decades. They are highly promoted by states' leagues and associations of cities and towns. These associations have an agenda to *help* rural communities catch up with the rest of the world and live in *modern* communities, where everything, including business, is orderly, well planned, new looking, and aesthetically pleasing. The goal of the sponsors of such ordinances, among other things, is to re-create towns where people don't have to worry about such serious things as unkempt home businesses, homemade signs, flies, unpleasant odors, and noisy farm animals at dusk and farm equipment at dawn. In the process legislatures and other ruling bodies violate inalienable, individual property rights, including freedom of choice.

Although Rosie was well educated and worked in the city, she liked the community the way it was. She had chosen to live there for a reason. She valued her property rights and freedom of choice. She respected her neighbors. And she recognized governmental abuse and infringement of fundamental property rights when she saw it. When, despite much opposition, the town council adopted the new ordinance, Rosie and a band of motivated citizens—we'll call them the Take Back Government (TBG) group—quickly gathered the signatures necessary to file a citizens' referendum petition, seeking to overturn the new law by vote of the people. But, it was questionable whether the citizens would be able to move forward with the referendum based on a recent change in state law.

The constitutionality of those new statutory changes, however, was being litigated and tested in an adjoining county. There, voters had sought to change the county land-use ordinance by citizen initiative to address concerns raised by proposals to construct two new power plants. Because of the timing and importance of the issue, the case was fast-tracked to the state supreme court. When the court ruled, it found the new state statute, which prohibited voters from petitioning for an initiative or referendum with respect to changes in local land-use ordinances, to be unconstitutional under the state constitution, which expressly provided for direct citizen legislation by initiative or referendum. Finally, four years into the fight for property rights in their community, Rosie and her group were encouraged. They had been working to preserve and protect their property rights for four long years.

Four years proved to be a magical number. The ordinance had been put on the table right after the last municipal election, when the mayor was reelected. Although the mayor and members of the planning commission had been working on the new ordinance behind the scenes for a year or so before that, it was presented *after* the election so that even if it did create a stir, the mayor hoped there would be plenty of time for the dust to settle before election time came around again four years later. But now the term had passed, and three council members as well as the mayor, who had then been in office for nearly twenty years, were up for reelection.

When the little group of citizens met early in the spring to plan their efforts regarding the referendum, Nick Romero said: "This is the year we get to close the deal. This is the year we can completely change the political landscape in this town. This is the year we have the opportunity to take back city hall and elect new leaders who won't just go back to the drawing board and do it all over again."

The group immediately set to work on a plan. They clearly defined their objectives and listed the steps they thought would be required to accomplish them. They defined two priority objectives: (1) win the referendum election; and (2) elect a new mayor and two new council members who would vote to protect individual liberties rather than trample them. Then they took an unusual step. They had come from diverse religious backgrounds, but they agreed to kneel in prayer about their undertaking. They prayed to a common God, their immortal Creator, the God of heaven and earth, the God of nature. After that, they repeatedly prayed, individually and collectively, about how they should recruit candidates to run for office. Then, after doing due diligence and based on the impressions they had received, they made a list of names of solid, electable members of the community who shared their ideology and would do a good job on the council. After praying again, they set about interviewing their choices and recruiting them to run for office.

When appealing to the would-be candidates, TBG group members weren't shy about explaining their approach and the fact that they had sought divine guidance. And they made promises and commitments of their own. They told the potential candidates that this was going to be an

Stories about People who have Walked the Walk—Making a Difference for Good

election process unlike any other this little town had ever experienced in the past. They would do much of the campaigning, host meet-the-candidate nights, sponsor debates, and even start a small-town newspaper to create a forum for discussion and help get the candidates' messages out. In short, they committed to working alongside their candidates to get them elected. Their commitment and enthusiasm was catching, and key, principled candidates were persuaded to run for office.

The group's next step was to start a small monthly newspaper in advance of the primary election so that it would be running in full swing when it was needed. It focused on stories of local interest. Printing costs were a sacrifice for those who published it, and again, success came down to a small group of persistent people. Spouses and primarily children of the group became the reporters, editors, and editorial board. They held contests to name the paper and get people interested, and they covered local news and information. People loved it.

A questionnaire to candidates running in the upcoming primary election was printed in the paper with their responses. A week before the election, the paper sponsored a meet-the-candidates night and candidate debate. With free hotdogs, drinks, and cupcakes provided, the event was well attended. While people were eating, they wrote questions for the candidates on note cards and put them in a box. All the candidates had an opportunity to introduce themselves, and an objective moderator posed the questions to the candidates.

"I believe the most important issues for our town government are: (1) honesty, transparency, and accountability in government; and (2) protecting individual rights and liberty," wrote the new mayoral candidate. Other responses from citizen-selected candidates were just as encouraging. "My vision for our town is a town where people have learned more fully the basic principles of human decency, live that way, and then mind their own business," said one. Another wrote: "In my opinion, residing and owning property is enhanced when self-determination is not curtailed. One's unfettered right to use property, unless it infringes upon another's use or is a safety risk, is an integral part of the pursuit of happiness." And another declared: "My view of the role of government is for it to protect all people's God-given rights of life, liberty, and the pursuit of happiness, and then to stay out of the way." Responses from the new candidates made it clear that the abiding incumbents were no longer the only game in town.

All the work and effort paid off, and the results of the primary election were what the TBG group had hoped for. They came away from the primary with their mayoral candidate and three council candidates still in the hunt. The referendum process, however, proved to be thornier. The sitting mayor and two council members did everything in their power to thwart the process. After twenty years in office, the mayor had come to run the town as if it were his own little kingdom, paying scant attention to the laws that stipulated the way he and the council could conduct their business. There was a history of plenty of collusion and behind-the-scenes scheming. But the ability to report it in the paper added a whole new level of accountability that had never existed before.

According to applicable laws governing citizen referenda, the town council was required to prepare and send out a neutral and unbiased voter information pamphlet. The town attorney came up with an introductory statement. The mayor then took responsibility for preparing the *for* argument while the TBG group of citizen sponsors took responsibility for the *against* argument. When the "unbiased" pamphlet came out, the "for" argument was printed in a larger font and had a large watermark "FOR" running diagonally across the page. The *against* argument was in a smaller font, with no watermark.

The TBG group addressed the unfair and unlawful presentation of the biased voter information pamphlet at a town meeting, but to no avail. A majority of the council, including the mayor and his two councilors, remained unmoved. So Nick asked, "If the laws of this state establish a certain process and procedure that a town must follow with respect to a referendum, specifically including the requirement that the town prepare and send out an unbiased voter information pamphlet, why should the council be entitled to make and enforce more laws that apply to everyone else while completing ignoring and thumbing its nose at the laws that govern the council's own operation?"

A majority of town council members were decidedly against the TBG group and had no feeling of responsibility toward them as constituents. The incumbents' next move was to launch a massive lawn sign campaign supporting the proposed ordinance and to organize a collaborative effort to split the vote in the council race in the general election. The TBG group was not deterred, however, and made a concerted effort to unite their support for the strongest of their candidates. Before the general election, the three remaining TBG candidates met and determined among themselves which of them was probably the most electable. As a result, one dropped out in order to unite their efforts and avoid splitting votes.

During a subsequent candidate debate just before the general election, the group's mayoral candidate received a standing ovation after he said:

"I am running on the platform of returning government to the people. . . . I don't think we need more laws. I think we need to learn how to get along with each other. I believe we should teach people correct principles and then basically stay out of the way and let them govern themselves. Many of the founders and former residents of this community were self-sufficient farmers and ranchers who built the town and made it the community it is today. . . . One of the big reasons they were the kind of people they were was because of their agricultural roots. . . . They understood the laws of nature and the law of the harvest. They had learned that you can't 'cheat the soil.' Based on their experiences with Mother Nature, they learned that they couldn't cheat and cut corners and get away with it. They knew that they would get out what they put in. . . . And rather than having a bunch of laws telling them everything they could and couldn't do, they exercised common sense, learned to get along, and learned how to resolve most of their own problems. . . . Many people today are far enough removed from these basic principles that they don't understand this—and it shows.

"With respect to Proposition 1, I'm not going to waffle—I'm against it! I will never voluntarily surrender my God-given property rights to any governmental entity, whether it be elected, appointed, or otherwise. I'm just not going to do it."

Besides the mayoral candidate and Rosie McLayne, one of the many heroes in this story is Nick Romero—a proud but humble God-fearing second-generation American citizen. Throughout the time of this referendum battle for property rights, Nick's wife was attending nursing school and working while Nick was holding down the fort at home despite his disabilities. Money was tight, but they lived as frugally and self-sufficiently as possible. In their backyard, Nick and his children tended a small flock of chickens as well as a garden, from which they bottled and preserved produce.

Nick's plate was plenty full at home, and he had never been particularly interested or involved in government or politics at any level—until he read a copy of the newly proposed land-use ordinance. When he read the proposed ordinance, he felt something deep inside say to him, "This is wrong and you need to do something about it." What was the local government trying to do in this little farming community? Such a proposal didn't even sound like the same America his parents had made such sacrifices to immigrate to!

Nick was a mainstay in the citizen-led effort. Despite all the other challenges and demands in his life, from meals to soccer games to PTA, he stepped up to the plate over and over again. Following his lead, his children got involved as well. They wrote for the paper and eventually took over primary editing and publishing duties. Nick hosted and emceed candidate debates, created thought-provoking lawn signs, stuffed envelopes, and knocked on doors. When, at the last minute, the TBG group decided to send out one last mailer just before the election, it was Nick and Rosie who spent half the night printing and preparing the mailer so that it would arrive in mailboxes the Saturday morning before the election.

When the general election finally happened the following Tuesday, there was an unprecedented 96 percent voter turnout! Freedom and liberty won the election, and the town voted down the new zoning ordinance by a margin of three to one. Perhaps even more important, the TBG group achieved all its other objectives, with the town electing the candidates the group supported by wide margins. Through a major team effort, the town reaped big dividends. Rosie, Nick, and others of like mind had stood up to be counted and made a big difference in the process. When it was all over, they recognized the hand of Divine Providence in their undertaking.

A few important points need to be emphasized here. None of these people ran for political office. They were not professional marketers or paid campaign managers. They challenged the law. They recruited, supported, and campaigned for the candidates. They did what they could where they were. This example again proves the 80/20 rule. The only thing 80 percent of the people in the whole community did was vote. Less than 20 percent did at least 80 percent of the work. Of the whole community, only about 20 percent of the entire population took *active* stands on either side of the issue.

There is little doubt that if the TBG citizens' group had not done what it did, the law would have remained in effect and the incumbent mayor and council would have remained in place. In the overall scheme of things, it may seem like a small difference in a small town, but in their lives and their town, the difference was huge. It is the kind of difference everyone needs to make if we are going to return America to her roots and enjoy the resultant "life, liberty, and the pursuit of happiness" that are our rights!

In addition to our desire to help educate and wake up *everyone,* we are specifically and actively seeking to reach out to the 20 percent—those who are willing to actually stand up and *do* something. As our friend Worth says, "As a general rule, the vast majority of people aren't interested in really getting educated; they just want to be stroked." Though that may be the general rule, we know there are exceptions to the rule. We are actively reaching out to those exceptions.

Engineering and Coordinating the Political Demise of a Fiscally Irresponsible U.S. Senator

Prior to 2010, this next story would have been truly remarkable. It still is, but this year, through the efforts of the Tea Party and others, it's not the only story of its kind. So far, though, this has been a banner year for political upsets. With the number of incumbent politicians defeated so far, we could probably talk about any of them, but the story we're going to tell is a little different than most.

It is well known that millions of dollars are typically spent on U.S. Senate races these days. For the most part, the names and places have been changed in the stories we use in our essays, so we'll call the U.S. senator who is the subject of this story Senator Bobb, a powerful multi-term senator with a political machine and a multimillion-dollar campaign war chest who seemed to have an absolute lock on reelection. Among other things, virtually all other elected leaders in the state were intimidated by him—by his finances, his political machine, and by some of his tactics. In fact, although one prominent elected leader in his own party announced early on that he would challenge Bobb for his Senate seat, it didn't take him long to bow out, leaving complete unknowns as the only opposition.

From our perspective, it was time for Bobb to go anyway, because, after four terms, he had been in office long enough. But in many voters' minds, he had been doing a reasonable job representing his constituents—until it came time to vote on TARP, healthcare, and other federal government bailout, and economic stimulus legislation. Then Senator Bobb crossed the line. When he drank the Kool-Aid, bought the pitch, and exercised the degree of fiscal irresponsibility necessary to vote for those programs, it really riled some of his constituents, including Doug Ketchum.

Up to that point, Doug had not been particularly concerned about or involved in government or politics, but in his words, he was "starting to wake up to what was going on." He was a busy entrepreneur and small-business owner, and his plate was plenty full. But as a talented auto mechanic and body and fender man, he had a side business restoring vintage cars, muscle cars, and hot rods. Of course, vintage car restorations aren't everyone's cup of tea, but when the markets were in a full upward swing from 2003 to 2007, there was a strong demand for his work. Even those who weren't in the market for one of his cars seemed to appreciate and enjoy looking at them. By early 2009, Doug had a good grasp of basic market dynamics, including supply, demand, credit, and a tightening money supply, and he could feel the effects of these things in his businesses.

Regardless of his previous lack of involvement in politics, Doug was concerned about the economy, but he was becoming even more concerned about increasing government spending. Because of his concerns, he went from politically inactive to Tea Party activist almost overnight and became one of the first Tea Party organizers in his state. And as he started paying closer attention to how Senator Bobb was voting on spending bills, he concluded, "Bobb's gotta go." Others felt the same way, including 9/12 activists, who had already been concerned about what was going on.

As Doug began meeting and aligning himself with others who shared similar concerns, he attended a rally that was intended to unify a wide variety of concerned citizens and political action groups from around the state under one common umbrella organization. In Doug's words, "The meeting—what was supposed to be a unifying rally—was a freaking joke. . . . You had all these people arguing over nothing. They all thought they were right about everything and wanted to be in charge."

Anyone who has been involved in this sort of thing can relate. Doug's next observation was particularly insightful and amusing: "They were trying to write a mission statement and spent over an hour in a heated argument about whether the terminology should be phrased '*in*alienable rights' or '*un*alienable rights.'"

At that point, Doug stood up and said, "You guys can argue and fight about nothing if you want to, but this is a joke." Then he walked out. Several people he didn't even know followed him. While the rest of the group stayed and argued over inconsequential trivia and who should be in charge, Doug and the others who walked out went across the street to a diner, got a booth, and started the process of devising an action plan that would actually make something happen.

Almost none of them had any previous involvement or experience with the political system. But they seemed to share a common vision about what was wrong with the nation: (1) an out-of-control federal government, (2) out-of-control government spending, (3) complete lack of fiscal responsibility, and (4) the need to reassert states' rights. One member of the group, a woman named Charla, did know something about their state's party caucus and nomination systems.

As they discussed what they wanted to accomplish, their highest priority was to take a strong stand on fiscal responsibility and to fire a shot over the bow of all their state's elected leaders by ending Senator Bobb's tenure in the U.S. Senate. At the time, the general election for his seat was almost eighteen months away, but there was going to be a whole lot of political wrangling going on in the meantime. Over the course of the next year, this group of concerned citizens evolved into a solid core group of eight people who shared a common vision and were committed to doing something about it.

Many told this small group that what they were trying to do was a pipe dream. It could not be done. Senator Bobb was far too powerful and had too much money.

When a prominent aspiring state politician from Bobb's own party announced early on that he would challenge the incumbent senator for his seat, Doug's group wisely held back and didn't jump on the bandwagon. With a massive campaign war chest and a lot of experience in all aspect of politics, Bobb quickly maneuvered to get an angle on his opponent and *persuade* him to withdraw before the campaign even became a race. Then a handful of others from Senator Bobb's party announced that they would likewise run for his seat.

The fact that there was so much interest in Bobb's seat within his own party showed that there was indeed some discontent and that perhaps Bobb might be vulnerable. But Bobb's competitors were virtually all political unknowns, with no significant political experience or campaign funding. No one thought any of them stood a chance. Any objective odds-maker would have been willing to bet big money that Bobb would retain his seat and claim his fifth term in the U.S. Senate. Still, Doug's group chose not to endorse or jump on board with any of the other candidates. Their focus was solely on Bobb.

As they studied and discussed the process, they determined that if they would effectively organize, their best chance of ousting Bobb was at the state party convention before even going to a primary election. According to party rules, Bobb would have to be one of the top two vote-getters at the state convention to go the primary, and if he secured 60 percent or more of the vote, there wouldn't even be a primary. This was going to take some serious planning, organization, and effort—and perhaps even a miracle.

Doug's unique and diverse group started holding Tea Party rallies. They started out small and built steadily. They provided refreshments of punch and cookies, brought balloons and banners, and recruited state and local politicians to come speak. They recruited the best speakers they could find. If any of their speakers were unprepared or didn't do a great job, they were not invited back. They learned how to *do* events as they went along.

One of the defining moments in their campaign came as they were planning a rally. There was a lot going on, and it was uncertain whether they could pull off the rally. Their group of eight equals, with no president, no chairman, and no clearly defined leader, voted five to three to go forward with the rally despite the challenges. At the appointed time, everyone, including those who had voted against it and had to change plans and schedules, showed up to make it happen. It was another success, and it kept them on track.

Their events became the functional equivalent of old-fashioned tent revivals. Doug would bring in one or more of his beautifully restored vintage cars to park right outside the front door as an attraction. The cars were a great icebreaker. Everyone seemed to want to look at and talk about the old cars. When reporters came, the cars were always the focal point of discussion. Acting as the spokesman for the group, Doug would usually end up talking more about cars than politics, avoiding most contentious political discussion. The old cars seemed to help make Doug and his associates seem more like the normal people they were rather than the fanatical weirdos that many wanted to portray them to be.

Their events kept getting bigger and bigger and better and better. In the meantime, they amassed an e-mail list with more than twenty thousand names and addresses. They utilized every component of social media, from Facebook to YouTube to Twitter in their recruiting efforts. They used a one-two punch approach. The events were intended to recruit, excite, and motivate people. Continual e-mail correspondence was their primary means of education.

Their objective was to recruit and train the right people to become delegates for the 2010 state party convention from all over the state.

Those delegates would be chosen at neighborhood party caucuses in early spring 2010, prior to the state party convention. To help educate and train the recruits, the activists held neighborhood caucus training sessions in every county in the state. They even held a mock state party convention so that by the time the *real* state party convention rolled around, all *their* delegates would know what they were doing and what to expect and do every step of the way. More than ten thousand people from all over the state showed up at the mock state convention! At that point, the group essentially knew that what they had set out to do was not only possible but also well within their grasp. Almost six months before the actual convention, they were confident that they would have enough delegates to block Bobb's candidacy and oust him at the state convention. They never endorsed another candidate, stating instead that they would be satisfied with any of them over Bobb.

In multiple media interviews during the weeks prior to the state convention, Doug expressed absolute certainty that they would be successful in ending Bobb's Senate career. By then, Senator Bobb and his team were in an absolutely frenzied panic, trying to play catch-up. They could read the writing on the wall.

The state convention ended up being anticlimactic. Everyone except those in absolute denial knew what was going to happen. Eight tenacious, hardworking, everyday people, with nothing but a vision, a plan, and a lot of effort, engineered and coordinated the political demise of a powerful, multiterm U.S. senator with a multimillion-dollar campaign war chest. Senator Bobb's Senate tenure unofficially ended almost six months prior to the 2010 general election, when he was to have secured his fifth term in the Senate.

Recognizing that a U.S. Senate campaign often consumes millions of dollars, a reporter once asked this group about their own budget. They laughed. They didn't even have a budget. Everyone in the core group had made big financial sacrifices to make this happen. Although they had received a few donations, their campaign was based on hard work, organization, and determination, not extraordinary financial resources. In the end, an obviously flustered Senator Bobb expressly admitted in a television interview following the state convention that this group with no money had overwhelmed his organization and resources.

Although you may disagree with what the group did and how they did it, we should all be tipping our hats to the fact that *they did it.* They got off their seats and did something. They figured out the system and worked within the system to effect a huge change. Their success is a living testament that it can be done. The more important point is—anyone can do this. Success is not always dependent on experience, power, or financial resources. If it were, this story would have turned out differently.

Pioneering New Frontiers in Independent Ballot Access

Our next story is about the growing interest in this country in independent politics and the issue of ballot access. Charlie Adams is a well-respected black American doctor, with several small business ventures on the side. Similar to Doug Ketchum, over the course of the past year or so, Charlie had awakened not only to the realities of our current situation in the United States but also to the realities of the situation with respect to the two major political parties. He could clearly see that the major parties had been essentially equally responsible for getting us into the mess we're in, that neither of the parties was likely to lead us out of it, and that neither of the parties really represented his political positions.

Although Dr. Adams was starting to feel internal motivation to get involved and do something, he was further motivated when he was approached by a group of people asking him to get involved by running for public office. At first he thought about running for state assembly, but in order to have any hope of providing the leadership necessary to effect the kinds of changes he felt like were necessary, he was persuaded to run as an independent candidate for governor. He would be the first black candidate for governor in his state. But according to state laws, in order to gain ballot access as an independent candidate for state-wide office, he would have to secure at least five thousand signatures on a petition to have his name placed on the ballot. Securing five thousand signatures was no small task, and state law required that the signatures be gathered in a short time period prior to the filing deadline for other major party candidates.

One of Charlie's acquaintances, Seth Miller, had essentially pioneered an electronic signature-gathering process via the Internet for other types of petitions. In studying statutory requirements, Seth concluded that existing laws should not preclude Dr. Adams from gathering signatures electronically for his independent candidacy. At first the state lieutenant governor, with responsibility for overseeing elections, indicated that the electronic signatures would be acceptable, so Charlie and Seth started gathering signatures—both paper and electronic. Between the two sorts of signatures, with a lot of help, they secured the five thousand signatures needed. At that point, the lieutenant governor reversed his position and refused to accept the electronic signatures. It was then too late to gather enough paper signatures to meet the statutory requirements.

By then Seth was heavily vested in the process, and he and Charlie were essentially partners in the endeavor. Ballot access by means of electronic signatures had become a matter of principle with Seth. They talked to several attorneys about their options for challenging the lieutenant governor's decision, but all the attorneys acted queasy about the case, wanted big retainers, and didn't act as though they could really jump right on it and make something happen. They all wanted to initiate an action at the trial court level and go from there. Similar to most attorneys, they acted more interested in seeing how they could complicate things, *work* the system, and see how much money they could collect from their clients.

At that point, Charlie was discouraged and seriously considered throwing in the towel. Although he wanted to do what he could to make a positive difference, he already had plenty on his plate, and he had neglected his medical practice, other business ventures, and family as he pounded the pavement to gather signatures. Plus, many in Charlie's own black American community thought he was already trying to play way over his head. What chance did he really have to get elected governor anyway? And many were disappointed that he had not carried the flag of tradition by running as a Democrat.

But Charlie's partner, Seth—a bold, unintimidated pioneer—was just getting his second wind. His main stake in the whole venture was to legitimize e-signatures for ballot access, and he was determined to test the limits under the law, even if it meant a court fight. Taking what all the attorneys had said with a grain of salt, Seth made a quick self-study of applicable laws and procedural requirements. He concluded that because the matter involved ballot access in a statewide election, they had direct recourse to the state supreme court. Then, acting as his own lawyer in a legal process that is beyond the experience and capability of many seasoned attorneys, Seth prepared and filed the necessary paperwork with the state supreme court to challenge the lieutenant governor's decision. As a matter of form, his paperwork might not have been perfect, but its basic substance was solid. If the court was willing focus on what really counted, he was confident they had a good case. His efforts rejuvenated Charlie's spirits, and they were back in the harness again, pulling together as a team.

Apparently the suit made the state quite nervous because the attorney general assigned a crack team of his best attorneys to respond to the filing. They threw the book at Seth and Charlie, seeking to disqualify Seth and have the case dismissed, and burying them with an avalanche of briefs, motions, and court filings, raising every imaginable issue, no matter how minute or inconsequential. It was another David versus Goliath matchup. Charlie and Seth sincerely prayed for help. And while Seth scrambled to attempt to keep up with the state's filings and paperwork, Charlie was eventually able to attract the attention and recruit the assistance of a well-funded, nonprofit, civil rights action group that was willing to retain a well-qualified attorney to take over the case and handle the oral argument.

Based on the circumstances and on the timeframe of the political race, the court agreed to handle the case on an expedited basis. A matter that could have otherwise been tied up in the legal system for years and cost Charlie and Seth hundreds of thousands of dollars in legal fees went from start to finish before the state supreme court in less than sixty days. Following oral argument and supplemental briefing, the parties waited with bated breath for the court's ruling.

In a precedent-setting ballot-access decision, the court unanimously reversed the lieutenant governor's decision and ruled that electronic signatures were legally sufficient for independent ballot access. It was a major legal victory for the cause of independent politics. Although the November election is now still weeks away and it's hard to say what Charlie's chances are, at least he's on the ballot.

Taking on the Federal Government

In our next story, we shift our attention back to the federal government and the relationship between the federal government and the states. In this account we're not even going to attempt to change the names or places. On one hand, it is a fairly well-known story. Books have been written about it. On the other hand, not near enough people have heard the story or read the books. It involves Sheriff Richard Mack and the landmark but little known U.S. Supreme Court case *Printz & Mack v. United States,* which we referred to earlier.

Cutting right to the chase, when the Brady Bill, the first serious stab at gun control by the federal government, was passed by Congress and signed into law by President Bill Clinton in 1994, Richard Mack was the sheriff of Graham County, Arizona. Regardless of your position on gun control—and Sheriff Mack has said he was not necessarily a big gun rights advocate at the time (he wasn't even a hunter)—the principle at issue in this case was not about guns but about the federal government's right and power to tell the states what to do.

According to language in the Brady Bill legislation, county sheriffs and local law enforcement were *mandated* to enforce the new federal law. Congress was telling county sheriffs what they had to do without providing any tools, funding, or resources to do so. But regardless of the tools, funding, or resources, the real question was whether Congress and the federal government had the power to tell county sheriffs what to do and whether the feds could force state and local governments and officials to do it. It was a question that had been simmering in this country for well over one hundred years, and most people had become convinced and just took for granted that Congress and the federal government are so powerful that they can tell anyone what to do and force them to do it. Few people had the backbone to challenge that position. But Sheriff Richard Mack was one of them. He ended up sacrificing his job, his office, and his career in law enforcement to challenge the new law and take on the federal government.

The case took almost three years to wind its way through the system, and it cost hundreds of thousands of dollars in legal fees. Fortunately, others stepped up to the plate and chipped in on the costs. Finally, in a landmark Tenth Amendment decision issued on July 27, 1997, the U.S. Supreme Court ruled that the Brady Bill was unconstitutional on the basis that and the federal government did not have the right, power, or authority to tell state and local officials what they had to do or to attempt to force them to do the federal government's bidding. Justice Antonin Scalia, writing for the majority, said, "The Federal Government may not compel the states to enact or enforce a federal regulatory program."

This was great news for Americans—news that many seem to have never heard or have long since forgotten.

Chapter 8

Lessons Learned and What We All Can Do

What is a common, recurring theme in all of the above stories? There are no quick, easy fixes! It doesn't just happen! It takes work. It takes effort. It takes time! It doesn't happen over night. People have to stand up and do something. It takes vision, organization, and coordination. But these stories also show what is possible—that we *do* have the power to make a difference.

In addition to lessons learned about rolling up our sleeves and getting involved, putting principles over politics, and the justifications for term limits, another important point we must understand is that today's Progressives have persuaded us to take our eyes off the most important level of government. And their philosophies and agendas have infiltrated state and local governments as well as public policy.

Over the past twenty years, many city ordinances have taken on the look and feel of homeowners' covenant contracts that limit property rights and claim control in areas that government has no right to operate. Ordinances have been put in place that have turned even local government away from the people, strong-arming rights of property and liberty into the hands of government officials. It has been done following the lead of an out-of-control federal government, all while we were simply living life and supporting our families, busy and distracted, focusing our attention on political issues only when covered by the mainstream media and its spin.

The situation in which we now find ourselves in the United States is precarious. Financially, we're situated in such a way that we're approaching the end of an unsustainable financial cycle, and we're going to have no choice but to start a new cycle. Politically, our governments—particularly the federal government—are out of control in scope of power and influence. Individually and collectively, we have drifted far from obeying the bedrock laws of nature and nature's God. As a direct result, the foundations of our great country, including the political and financial systems have become cracked and broken. The situation is serious, but it can be corrected—just not with more Band-Aids.

We have reached a point, however, as reiterated in *Prosperity!,* where we're going to need help—*divine help*—to turn things around. Just as our forefathers relied on divine intervention to accomplish the impossible and win independence from the British during the Revolutionary War, we need that help now, and we will need it even more in the future. While some may not recognize the true gravity of our situation, eventually they will. And just as George Washington and his army were reduced to utmost humility and the pits of despair in Valley Forge before the tide turned, in all likelihood we will have similar experiences. And just as with General Washington and his troops, and Matt James and others, in the end such experiences will be for our good.

Recognizing an old adage that "God helps those who help themselves," there is another saying that in order to qualify for the divine help we need, we should work as though it were entirely up to us but pray as though it were entirely up to God! At this point, we would be well advised to take heed and begin that process because the situation can be fixed; similar situations have been fixed in the past. But it is up to us—we the people. We are the only ones who, with divine help, can fix things. But first, after turning our backs on Deity for so long, we've got to quit turning our backs on God, and get our Divine Creator, the God of Nature, back on our side, and back in our country.

We All Can Do This

The examples and success stories shared above are just a few examples of what people have done. These people and many others are doing what it takes to help take back their communities. We can all do what Nick and Rosie and Doug and Charlie have done, starting at the foundation and working from the bottom up. As Matt James says, "The first thing to do is just catch the vision and run with it." It's the "run with it" part—the action part—that stops most people. Taking action is the first hurdle.

After getting God back in our personal lives and reconnecting to the bedrock of our existence, we need a three-prong approach as it relates to our government. The first, most important, level to focus on is the foundational level, with an emphasis on personal responsibility and community, returning to the bedrock of the laws of nature and of nature's God. Second, we need to focus attention on strengthening and taking back the states by saying no to the ever-imposing federal government and its numberless, needless agencies. We need to correct laws against Deity and liberty that permit local governments to trample personal liberty and property rights. The biggest problems at the state level often begin with collusion between people/business and government. Finally, and simultaneously, we need to begin to address the abuses of the federal government, getting back to the constitutional limits that the federal government has come to ignore. Simply stated, we need to *say Enough!*

One state governor recently said that his biggest challenge is "fighting the federal government in its efforts to absolve anyone and everyone of their personal responsibility." We need to step up and *take* personal responsibility. We need to be proactive and take this country full cycle—forward to the founding principles on which it was based, principles enumerated in the Declaration of Independence, the Constitution, and the Bill of Rights: "the Laws of Nature and of Nature's God."

This is something we all need to do. The good news is that it is up to us; we can make it happen. The more people who stand up in this country, the stronger it will be. We all need to do what we can, wherever we are, to lift where we stand. It's all a part of strengthening the foundation, building from the bottom up, and moving forward to a solid new vision and reality.

We affirm that ultimately lasting freedom, peace, and prosperity come from adhering to "the Laws of Nature and of Nature's God!"

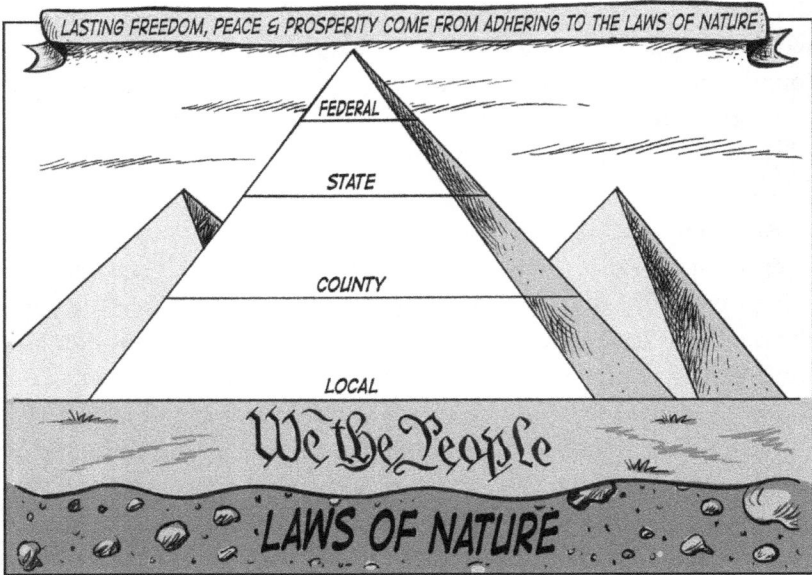

www.ingramcontent.com/pod-product-compliance
Lightning Source LLC
Chambersburg PA
CBHW022112280326
41933CB00007B/359